Though the Storms Rage

Yet Will I Dance

Marion Kilchester

Though the Storms Rage Yet Will I Dance

Copyright © 2020 Marion Kilchester

Published by Disruptive Publishing
    with permission from Marion Kilchester

        17 Spencer Avenue
        Deception Bay QLD 4508
        Australia
        www.disruptivepublishing.com.au

Edited by Nola Passmore (www.thewriteflourish.com.au)

Formatted for print and eBook by Snowflake Productions

Cover art by Timothy Kilchester

First published 11.11.2020

All Rights Reserved. No part of this publication may be reproduced, distributed or transmitted in any form, or by any means, including photocopying, recording, or any other electronic methods, without the prior written permission of the publishers. Brief quotations that are credited to the publication and the author are permitted.

ISBN # 978-0-6489671-4-9

To those who have gone before me.

My mother, Connie (Constance) Ellicott-nee Brown. I have no memory of you and yet you shaped my life, handing to me your gift of music.

My 'adopted' mother, Lillian Pankhurst. You took me into your home when I was hurting. Most of who I am today, I owe to you.

My beautiful little daughter, Tabitha, gifted to me for nearly two years. Though your life was short, you gave me so much.

Kola, my beloved husband. You loved me and pushed me to extend myself. I owe you greatly and still miss you.

Contents

Introduction	7
Chapter 1 – Finding Me	9
Chapter 2 – Tabitha	51
Chapter 3 – Displaced	91
Chapter 4 – Into the Valley Again	121
Chapter 5 – What the Locusts Have Eaten	149
Chapter 6 – Forgiveness, Faith and a Future	199
Chapter 7 – Dancing Solo	217
Chapter 8 – Bridal Waltz	245
Author's Notes	265

Introduction

I had almost completed this book when I had a dream. As I pondered over its message, I knew that it was God-given and that it would be the introduction to my story. This, then is the dream.

A sleek, black pony shivered, as his trainer who had rescued him after a storm, stood beside him and directed a heavy jet of water onto his flanks. The memory of the fierce storm that had separated him from his mother was still vivid in his mind, the crashing thunder and the stinging rain.

As he grew, the memory of that storm and the resultant fear remained with him. His dance in the storm had not been one of exultant joy and excitement. Nor was it one of resigned passivity. He had been crazed by fear, as he attempted to escape his tormentor, the storm.

The trainer spoke gently as he released the rein and continued to direct the jet of water over the body of the pony. Apart from a small shiver every now and again, the pony did not flinch, but stood his ground, all the while listening to the calming voice of his rescuer. The pony had come a long way. He was learning to trust his trainer and in so doing, was losing his fear. He was learning to dance in the rain.

A little girl was standing nearby, watching the pony. She held a large key in her hand—one of those old ornate keys. As I looked from her to the pony and back again, I knew that she and her key were a significant part of this story.

Though the Storms Rage
Yet Will I Dance

I asked God, 'What is the key?' and He answered me by giving me a text:

'Let the little children come to me, and do not hinder them, for the kingdom of God belongs to such as these. I tell you the truth, anyone who will not receive the kingdom of God like a little child will never enter it.'

(Mark 10:14, 15; NIV)

I knew the answer to my question!

Little children will jump into their father's arms. If they have a good father, they will trust him to catch them and hold them safe.

The key to being able to dance in the rain, and not be afraid of the storm, is trust in God. He has and will continue to be with me through all the storms of my life, as He will with you, when you invite Him to walk with you through all the ups and downs of your life.

Here is the story of my life and how I learnt to dance in the rain.

Chapter 1 – Finding Me

1. The Open Box
2. Confronting with Truth
3. Different Kinds of Cold
4. Journey to a Sister's Embrace
5. The Road Behind
6. 'Cinderella' Reworked
7. The Next Ten Years

The Open Box

Could I break through that impenetrable wall of silence? Could I find me?

For nineteen years I had tried to find out about me, but I kept hitting that horrible wall. Why wouldn't anyone tell me the answers to my questions? I knew that I had a brother and a sister, but I did not know them. Each of us had been brought up by different people, in different homes and in different towns.

I sat in the hot cluttered farm shed. Boxes were lying all around me. My parents were hundreds of miles away. This was my opportunity to open those dusty cartons. They had been packed up and unopened for as long as I could remember. Somehow, I knew those packing cases were the key to solving my mystery.

Tears welled in my eyes as I realised what that long-sealed, dusty cardboard packing carton contained. Staring at the contents, all yellowed by age, I hoped that I was about to find the answer I was searching for. How long had this box been sealed? Twelve years? Twenty years?

My fingers trembled as I pulled out the first sheet. Piano music. No name. I drew out the second sheet. Still nothing. Pulling out the third sheet, I caught my breath as I stared at the name on the music – Lorna Watt. Quickly I pulled out more pieces of music–some were songs, others were piano pieces. Many bore the signature 'Lorna Watt'. Was this the answer for which I'd been searching?

By the time I was halfway through the box, however, the music had a different signature—Connie Brown'.

With the music now separated into two piles on the floor I slumped over the empty box. I was looking for one name but I had found two. My search had just become more complicated. I picked up the one name and then the other. Who were they and did either of them have any connection

Though the Storms Rage
Yet Will I Dance

to me? I didn't know what name I was looking for; just a name which could tell me who I was. My name was Marion Ellicott, but I didn't know who I belonged to. I believed my father was my natural father. We clicked. He played the banjo; I played the piano. We both loved and made music. Sometimes we would make music together. We both loved dogs and we both loved the farm and the wide-open spaces. Yes, I knew he was my Dad.

But my mother? We had no connection. Nothing. We were like enemies. We fought. There were never any kind words, just cruel taunts, jibes and put-downs. She could never give me an answer to my many questions. Questions like, 'Did you breastfeed me? What did I look like when I was a baby? Do you have a photo of me as a baby?'

I traced each signature with the index finger of my right hand while wiping away tears with my left hand. Shaking my head, I asked myself, 'What have I uncovered here?' Even as I shook my head, I could not stop the excited tremors rippling through my body.

Carefully, I repacked the box, keeping out just two pieces – one with Lorna's name on it and the other with Connie's name.

Returning to the house where I was staying, I showed my find to my landlady, Mrs Silva, and told her of my lifelong search.

'I have a sister. I need to find her. I think she lives in Tumut, but I don't have her address or telephone number.'

After enquiries to Telecom's Phone Directory Assistance, we found a number, which we thought would be hers.

I'd had no contact with my sister, Dawn, for many years. Shaking, I dialled the number.

'Hello, this is Marion, your sister. I'm ringing from Tamworth.' There was a brief silence, before my sister replied.

'Marion? My little sister, Marion?'

Chapter 1 – Finding Me
The Open Box

'Yes – it's me.'

By then we were both crying.

'I've found sheets of music with two different names on them. Connie Brown and Lorna Watt. Can you tell me who these people are?' Again, silence.

'Marion, I can't answer that question. Where are you ringing from?' I told her. 'Put me on to the lady you are with.'

Handing over the phone, I swallowed hard and held back tears as a deep disappointment washed over me.

I'd come up against that solid brick wall again. Why won't anyone give me answers? After they talked for a while, the phone was handed back to me.

'Okay, you won't answer the first question. So, answer this question. Either you are not my sister, or my 'mother' is not my mother. Which is it?' Silence met me yet again. But this time, the silence had given me the answer.

'It's okay, I know that you are my sister. So, the question now is, which of those two women, whose names are on the music, is my mother?'

She hesitated, but a grim determination pressed me on. 'Who is my mother? Lorna Watt or Connie Brown?'

'Connie Brown is your mother, and mine.' The wall came down and the secrets of my life and past came tumbling out.

Confronting with Truth

When I found the sheet music in the box, I was staying with Mr and Mrs Silva, just a ten-minute walk from the farm where I had grown up. The boxes had been stored there for twelve years, ever since we had moved from Sydney to Tamworth, and I knew they would give me clues to my identity. It had been the perfect time to search because my parents were 116 km away. The day after I found the sheet music with the two different names written on them, Mr and Mrs Silva drove me to Boggabri where Dad was building a church.

I dressed carefully and spent extra time fixing my long black hair. I needed every bit of help I could get to take the next step. I prayed to my God to give me courage and the right words to say.

Mr and Mrs Silva, who had fostered many children during their lives, were the perfect backstops for me.

The closer we got to Boggabri, the more nervous I became. I closed my eyes and rolled and re-rolled my scarf around my fingers, wishing we were back in Tamworth. My throat was dry and tears I dared not shed prickled my eyes.

'Oh, God, I can't do this,' yet even as I breathed the words, I knew I had no choice. If I was to move on, then I must face them with my newfound truth.

When we arrived, I got out of the car, with my friends behind me. Dad saw us arrive and came to meet us. Everything in me wanted to turn and run, but I had come this far, so breathing deeply, I walked towards him and embraced him. I could not for my own sake drag this out by waiting for my stepmother, so I jumped straight to the point.

'I know the truth, Dad. I know who my mother is.' He stopped abruptly and stared at me before looking down and shuffling his feet. I

Though the Storms Rage
Yet Will I Dance

could tell he was shocked and didn't know what to do or say. By now, Mr and Mrs. Silva were standing either side of me, and we went into the caravan to tell my stepmum what I had just told Dad. I can't remember what her reaction was. I guess I don't need to.

Later, when I had Dad to myself, I asked him, 'Why did you lie to me, and why did you swear everyone else to secrecy also?' He stood silent for a while and then answered me,

'I just wanted to give you a proper home and a mother.'

I have never held bitterness towards either of them. Dad did what he thought he had to do. It was the wrong choice, and he married the wrong woman, but his motivation was right.

Different Kinds of Cold

Bitter cold clawed at me as I sat in the back row of the Town Hall. It was August 1966, and the eisteddfod was in progress. August in Tamworth, Australia is winter and the large brick hall with its high ceiling and balconies had no heating. Students waiting their turn to compete in the piano sections sat, cloaked in winter coats and scarves. Gloved hands clasped hot-water bottles wrapped in towels, trying to keep fingers warm enough to play their pieces well.

My students were competing in several sections during the competition and I needed to be there for them. As I sat in that back row, it wasn't just my hands and feet that were cold. A different kind of cold and numbness had settled in the core of my body as I grappled with the truth. After nineteen years of questioning and searching, I now knew who my mother was, but she was dead.

The brick wall of not knowing had come down, only to be replaced with a bigger, thicker wall. There wasn't even a headstone I could read and touch and wet with my tears. I learnt that she was buried in a graveyard in Sydney. Because Dad was very poor, he could not afford to buy a headstone. As he was a bricklayer, he built one instead. Much love and tears went into the building of that headstone, but the council would not allow it and removed it. There remained just a vacant plot of ground.

As I sat in that cold hall, I struggled to concentrate on my students as grief set in. Hot tears began to run down my face before I stood up and ran from the hall.

It was such a strange mix of emotions coursing through me: anger that everyone had lied to me for nineteen years and relief that the lady I had called Mum, but who had given me no love, was in fact, not my mum. There was excitement because I now knew where my love of music and the desperate need to play the piano came from. The hardest emotion of

Though the Storms Rage
Yet Will I Dance

all to deal with was the grief I felt for a mother I never knew and never would, this side of heaven. With the help of God, my friends, the family I was living with and sedatives from my doctor, I got through the eisteddfod week and was able to be there for my students.

Indeed, during that time I began to grow up and think more like an adult than a child or a troubled teenager. My students were my responsibility that week. I had to put them first. I needed to calm my nervous students and encourage them all to do their best. I needed to rejoice with them when they achieved and won awards, even while my heart was breaking.

Journey to a Sister's Embrace

A few days later, I stood on the platform waiting to board the train to Tumut. As the carriage was empty, I chose a window seat so I could watch the passing scenery and put my feet close to the heaters which ran along the wall. It was winter and the temperatures outside were cold.

The interior of the carriage was fitted out with polished wood and the overhead luggage racks were black wrought-iron. The atmosphere was one of old-fashioned elegance.

My journey required two changes—one at Sydney and another at Cootamundra. The journey was about 500 miles (about 800 km). Although travelling alone, I was not afraid. Excitement carried me forward on two fronts. Firstly, I had never travelled on a train before, but more significantly, I was on my way to get to know a sister I hadn't seen for twelve years. I was only seven when we were separated.

This was an adventure, and I was ready for it. The confrontation with my Dad and stepmum was behind me. So too was the eisteddfod. The train was to me, fit for a queen and in my lovely new clothes I felt like a princess.

I flitted from one side of the carriage to the other, drinking in the scenery and the ambience of the carriage as the wheels propelled me to a new season in my life.

The sooty smoke streamed past the window as though it was carrying the stresses of the past week, far away behind me.

As we rolled through the countryside to Tumut, the hills were golden with the full bloom of the Cootamundra wattle trees. The Cootamundra hills in August were incredibly beautiful. Fifty years on, I still remember what I wore on the journey. A blue and grey tartan-style skirt was topped with a blue and white striped jumper. White Bermuda socks

Though the Storms Rage
Yet Will I Dance

(up to my knees) and blue shoes completed my outfit. To keep me warm, I had a thick, light-sky-blue coat and white scarf. I didn't know it then, but my sister's favourite colour for clothes is blue.

As I neared Tumut, my stomach began to knot up. Would I recognise my sister? Would she recognise me?"

There were a lot of passengers on the last leg of my journey. When the train halted, the doors opened and people began to leave the train. Clutching my suitcase, I peered out the windows as I made my way to the door. There she stood with her husband beside her. Our eyes met, and for each of us there was no doubt as we ran to each other and embraced.

The Road Behind

When I opened the box, I found out who my mother was, but I found also, the name of a second woman. Who was she? Why was the music of both these women packed away, untouched for years? I had found the answer to the one question I'd been asking for years ('who was my mother?'), but now I found so many compartments yet to be unpacked, so many pages remaining to be read, so many pieces of the puzzle still to be put together.

That box became the vessel from which I unpacked not just my beginnings, but the lives, the hardships and tragedies, the successes and failures of many people. I unpacked a family.

Dad was only twenty-three when he first married. His wife, Lorna Watt, was seventeen. Lorna, a typist and an excellent pianist, was the owner of the rest of the music in the box. Lionel, their only child was born thirteen months later. Lorna developed an abscess on her brain and became very ill. She spent much time in the Royal Prince Alfred Hospital, Sydney, before passing away on 19 October 1930. She was only twenty-two. Lionel was just a little over three years old.

Dad coped with Lorna's death in the only way he knew how. He went to his parents and asked them to take Lionel into their home while he went out to the country to work. Jobs were hard to get due to the Depression. He worked as a bricklayer with a firm who built churches, convents and associated buildings.

He worked in towns such as Young, Wagga, Junee and Goulburn, so he did not have much opportunity to spend time with his young son.

Dad never forgot Lionel's birthday or Christmas. Lionel said, 'He always came home for my birthday and he came home for Christmas and he would stay. At Christmas, I think he stayed about two weeks and my birthday it was usually just for a weekend.' Those two weeks would have been the sum total of his annual leave.

In between visits, Lionel and Dad kept in contact by letters. You can see Dad's love for Lionel in the following letter:

'Dear Lionel,

I have been talking to Santa Claus & he gave me a Seaplane, a bugle, & a little house with a lot of little animals in it for you. There are two Sheep, two pigs, two donkeys, two dogs, & two moo cows & two Little girls to look after them for you. So get grandfather to get a flat Box about 2ft x 2ft to put them in so they won't get lost & dady [sic] will Bring them down to you at Christmastime. Now good bye with tons of love & kisses from your ever loving dady. [sic]

Xxxxxxx Keith'

The letters are full of childish exuberance and record the thoughts of a small boy away from his father. Always eager to show his father that he was trying hard at school, Lionel also shared his adventures with his father.

'Dear Daddy,

I received most welcome letter, and was glad to hear you were well and having a good time. You was [sic] clever daddy shooting so many rabbits with that old gun. I spent all the money you gave me before you left daddy except threepence. I bought two books to write and draw in at home for sixpence and a new bell for my bike. Please dear daddy will you send me 2/6 to get a lamp for my bike. I done[sic] well in my monthly test at school. I got 5 marks for writing, 7/10 Dictation, 30 out of 30 for arithmetic, 5½ Reading.

Well good night daddy with fond love and tons of kisses from your ever loving little mate Lionel.

Chapter 1 – Finding Me
The Road Behind

I Did miss you when you went away daddy.'

xxxxxxxxxxxxxxxx

'Dear daddy I wrote to you last night. But I have got some more news for you. I went to school and every sum was right and also got nort [sic] for Dictation in exam. In the after-noon the fun doctor came. We had three pennies worth of community singing and these are the songs. The first song was Today I feel so happy then the next was Who's afraid of the big bad wolf and the last song was there's an old Spinning wheel in the Parlour. After that he lit a big piece of paper nose. But after that he played the piano with his nose. But! After that he stood four chairs on his forehead. Good night Daddy'

Dad kept all of those letters as treasured memories.

Lorna had been a very good pianist, so when Lionel was seven, Dad organised for him to learn to play the piano also. When he was only eight years old, he played 'Here Comes the Bride', at the wedding of his Aunt Madge (his mother's sister). I can only imagine what effect that would have had on all present.

Dad continued to work away, travelling from town to town for seven years. A young waitress in a hotel in Goulburn won his heart and in 1937 Dad married Connie. Lionel was now ten years old. Returning to Sydney, Dad began building a new house for his family. Dawn was born in January 1939. In September of that year the house was completed and Lionel, now twelve years old, moved in with his dad and stepmother. Naturally there were teething problems, but never any abuse or cruelty. *As Lionel said: "Connie was Salvation Army and quite genuine about it – a very quiet sort of a woman. In retrospect, I think I gave her hell. I was a typical teenage rebel who didn't want a stepmother telling me what to do. So we had a few arguments before I got married, [but] we got to be quite good friends."*

Though the Storms Rage
Yet Will I Dance

Connie (my mother), Dad, Lionel and Dawn settled into a normal, happy family routine. It wasn't always plain sailing, however. Lionel recalls an instance when his little sister Dawn interfered with what he was doing *'so I tied her up to the rotary clothes line so she couldn't get to what I was doing and Connie and I had another argument over that'*.

Not long after Dawn was born, Connie developed kidney problems, chronic nephritis which plagued her for the rest of her life. I was born eight and a half years after Dawn, but never knew my mother. Her health was deteriorating, and Dawn and I spent a lot of time being cared for by our mother's parents and her sister, Aunty Marion, who I was named after. Connie fell pregnant again, not long after I was born. Because of her poor health and financial hardship, (they were poor, with the Depression hitting them quite hard) this pregnancy was not wanted. Someone gave Connie mercury tablets to abort the baby. The combination of the mercury tablets and the poor condition of her kidneys cost not only the life of the unborn baby but also that of my mother. After a long battle with illness Connie died just three weeks after her stepson Lionel's marriage to his teenage sweetheart, Joyce.

Dawn and I remained in the care of our grandparents and Aunty Marion for some time. As Aunty Marion had no children of her own, she made a bid to adopt us. Grandfather Brown advised Dad to marry again quickly, so that he could keep his family together and not lose his girls. He was burdened with grief over the death of his second wife, anxious about the whole horrible situation he was in, and struggling with typhoid fever.

Having lost out on nine years of his son's life, after the death of his first wife Lorna, he could see history beginning to repeat itself. He took on a housekeeper and brought Dawn back from Goulburn. The housekeeper, Ivy, was very sweet, treated Dawn well and was an excellent housekeeper. Dad married her and brought me home from Goulburn.

Ivy changed immediately after she was married. She told someone, 'you can sack a housekeeper. You can't sack a wife.' How she could even think that, I don't understand for she was a divorcee. Her first husband had

Chapter 1 – Finding Me
The Road Behind

walked out of the marriage and set up house with her brother's wife and moved from New South Wales to Victoria.

I was only two years old, cute with big eyes and Shirley Temple curls. Life must have been alright for me, pampered and dressed like a little doll. For my sister, life became hell. She was physically, mentally and emotionally abused.

Dad stood by and allowed it to happen. My sister was subjected to this abuse for five years, until she ran away from home at sixteen. Dawn fled to Goulburn where she received from Aunty Marion the love and care she craved and which had been denied her.

I shared a bedroom with my sister during those five years and must have witnessed much of what was happening, yet I have no memory of anything to do with family life during that time. My way of 'dancing in the rain' at that age was to blot it out of my memory. I do remember dancing classes and being dressed in a red and white polka dot dress, with cotton wool 'snow' around the hem. I remember Sunday School and a colouring-in book of children's prayers, which I loved very much.

My first teacher at school used to fill the chalkboard with beautiful, colourful pictures, illustrating the stories she told. I had a best friend, Beverley who lived just down the street. We shared our birthdays, school days, Sunday-school and physical culture classes. The memories I have are beautiful. The bad things are totally erased.

After researching my father's life, I found myself asking, 'What made the difference?' 'What changed him?' I drew four reasons for the changes in Dad.

He married his first two wives because he loved them. He married his third wife in haste out of a desperate bid to keep his children.

Brokenness from the loss of two wives and separation from his children, compounded by Connie's sister Marion's bid to adopt the girls, which would have caused further separation. This forced him into making a decision which ended with dire consequences.

He was a fiercely independent man, yet he became dependant on the third woman, and in so doing gave up who he was.

He was a scallywag by nature, possessing an innate sense of humour. This part of his character was destroyed by his third wife, Ivy. He became a puppet in the hands of this woman.

A combination of grief, fear of losing his children, illness (Dad had typhoid fever during the last few months of my mother's life), a cruel woman dictating life, friction in the family and years of struggle to make ends meet finally broke him, changing his personality until he had no fight left in him. He abandoned who he was and in so doing, abandoned his children.

He failed to protect us from abuse, and in Dawn's case, aided and abetted the abuse. Frustration and anger would have contributed to his character change.

Most of all, trying to cope with life in his own strength and wisdom, without input from God, caused him to fail.

As I learnt about my father's life, I shed buckets of tears.

A deep empathy and a deeper love for him developed, for by this time, I too had experienced loss several times over. My own losses enabled me to relate to his losses and his life struggles.

Sometimes you learn from the good example of others. Other times you learn from their mistakes.

I loved my Dad and grieved for a mother I never knew. I succeeded in life, despite an unloving stepmother, and learnt to 'dance both in sunshine and storm' with a God who sustains. I found me.

Cinderella Reworked

Two photos signpost the year my life changed.

The first photo shows a young, six-year-old girl. Her hair is long and thick, black and shiny with curls down to her shoulders. A big pink bow adorns her hair. She is smiling and has big brown eyes and rosy cheeks. She's dressed in a pink dress, trimmed with lace and ribbons, with white ankle socks and shiny black shoes. She looks like a little princess with the world at her feet.

In the second photo, she is seven years old. Her hair is now short. The curls are gone. She looks happy, dressed in a pink satin and tulle full-length junior bridesmaid's dress. Rosettes trim the full skirt. The bodice is pink brocade. Holding a posy of spring flowers, she still looks like a princess. She didn't know it then, but that day marked the end of her life as she knew it. That little girl was me.

Three events during the year after I turned seven marked the turning point in my life.

The first happening was my sister leaving home, just after my seventh birthday.

The second thing happened towards the middle of the following year, when my stepmother's niece, Jean asked if I could be junior bridesmaid at her wedding. With the help of a neighbour my stepmum got to work making me a beautiful dress and a matching warm fluffy cape to keep me warm. The wedding was in Armidale and I was showcased to all of her family.

It was probably during this trip to Armidale from Sydney that Dad found the farm at Tamworth. Soon after the wedding, the Sydney home was sold, and we relocated. This was the third event. Away from all of my father's family, my mother's family and far enough away from my stepmother's family, my 'mum' changed totally toward me.

My chores increased dramatically over time until I found myself caring for the young animals on the farm, hand feeding them, locking them up of a night-time and letting them out of a morning. I loved the animals, and this was a job I enjoyed doing. I also had to collect the eggs from seven hundred fowls, and then hand clean and box them. Because they were free range, the eggs were often dirty, coated with chook manure and mud, and sometimes the sticky remains from broken eggs. You couldn't immerse the eggs in water because that removed the natural preservative coating from the shell, so each egg needed to be carefully cleaned with a soft damp cloth. Then the eggs were packed into boxes provided by the marketing board. The boxes were labelled according to size, so as I cleaned, I graded and boxed.

Housework, even cooking meals, ironing, and darning my Dad's socks were added to my growing list of chores to be completed on a daily basis. I became my stepmum's little slave girl, with no remuneration or love given in return.

I didn't mind doing housework. It was the sheer volume of work, the unrealistic expectations and nastiness of my 'mum' which I hated. I gained satisfaction in a neat, tight darn completed on my Dad's sock. I loved everything to be neat, tidy and in place. I hated litter. Even to this day, I am the same.

My 'mum' was quite lazy and untidy. She hoarded stuff like tins, bottles and newspapers. Everything was piled on top of the benches. You would think I had enough to do as a child, but I remember waiting until my parents went away, which they frequently did, and I'd get into the kitchen and declutter, getting rid of unnecessary things and putting everything else inside the cupboards, leaving the table and bench tops free of stuff, clean and tidy. Needless to say, I would get punished for my efforts, but the tidy kitchen, for me, outweighed the punishment.

Chapter 1 – Finding Me
Cinderella Reworked

Once I remember my parents driving to a farm up on the Moombi Range. I came home from school, did my chores, and cooked myself sausages and vegetables. I cooked just enough for myself, washed up, did my homework and went to bed. They came home, and had to cook their own meal. Again, I was in trouble, but I didn't care. I had completed all my chores. The rest was their responsibility.

Because of the huge volume of housework, which I had to do, I struggled to get all my schoolwork completed. After I tried to explain what was happening to my teacher, she called a meeting with my parents. My 'mum' lied to the teacher and my Dad agreed with her. The teacher then accused me of lying and of laziness. I was and am not a liar or lazy, but there was nothing I could do about it. I just had to swallow hard and accept the injustice that life was dealing me.

I always had friends at school, but rarely could I have a friend home or go to my friend's home.

When I did get a friend home, or go to my friends' homes, the contrast between their lives and mine was huge. I knew they had something which I did not. I guess I knew they were loved and I was not.

As my high school friends spoke of family, especially mother/daughter relationships and shared activities, I was unable to join in. Those experiences were totally foreign to me. Although I was part of this circle, I felt so totally alone. I knew I was different, but didn't really know why. I didn't want to be different, but I was, and it hurt deep down inside.

Why didn't I have what my friends had? I had a mother, so why couldn't I relate to her? Why was it all so different? Why, indeed, was I so different? Slowly, insidiously, the 'being different' and feeling inadequate turned into a deep-seated feeling of inferiority. I lived in a different world. A chasm was widening before me, separating me from something which I desperately wanted. I began to ask questions, but never received any answers.

Though the Storms Rage
Yet Will I Dance

Occasionally there would be a breakthrough. I was elected class captain in Grade 5. In Grade 6, I won first place in a poster competition. As a teenager, I taught Sunday school, played the organ at church, became a leader at my Presbyterian Youth Fellowship. In the big picture, they were only shafts of light shining through rifts in the storm clouds, or maybe they were gifts, saying, 'Hang in there, girl – You are of worth'. Whichever way I took it, they helped me to dance in the storm.

There was always someone or something in my life, which provided specific needs, amidst the dark clouds.

I did not have wicked stepsisters. Instead I had an absent sister. A fairy godmother was not part of my story, but always there was someone or something, which fulfilled that role.

In primary school, I had Mrs Roberts. This beautiful lady, the wife of the boys' primary headmaster, was our school librarian. Another girl Susan and I became library monitors and spent lunchtimes and morning-tea times in the library with Mrs Roberts. She taught us how to stack the books correctly and to help with the monitoring in the library. Excitedly, we'd watch her open up new boxes of books and then we'd eagerly read through series upon series of books, such as the *'Cherry Ames-Nurse Series'*, the *'Billabong Series* 'and many others. Yes, I danced through those primary school years with the kindness and love of a very special librarian.

Another kind woman helped me in a very practical way.

'Cawoline, look a wabbit wan acwoss the wood'

Oh my! That doesn't sound very good. I was ten years old. I was intelligent, could spell and was an avid reader, but I couldn't speak very well. I could not enunciate certain words. I don't know whether Dad just accepted my speech as normal, or was too busy with his own life to take much notice of mine.

My stepmother certainly would not have helped me. But you know what? God heard me, and he provided the help I needed.

Chapter 1 – Finding Me
Cinderella Reworked

I attended Sunday school at St Andrews Kirk, Tamworth. The minister's wife, Mrs. Ross listened to my speech every Sunday, and decided something had to be done, and she was the one to do it. She approached my parents, 'Marion's speech is very poor, but I can help her. I am a speech therapist. Will you let her come to me once a week after school? It is free, I will not charge fees.'

My parents really could not say no, so weekly I went to Mrs. Ross and gently she worked with me, replacing 'w's with 'r's and correcting other speech defects. In my teens and early adult years, people would often ask me if I was English. I wasn't, but I had been taught how to enunciate words. Even now, there are words I have to think about as I say them, but Mrs. Ross did a great job.

I loved Sunday school. Each week we were given a picture with a memory verse written on it. We coloured in the picture and took it home to memorise the verse for the next week. After Sunday school, some of us stayed for the first part of the service. After the minister or someone told us a story, we'd sing a children's hymn and then go home. For that section of the service we would sit in the front of the church in the choir seats. Either way I was close to the pipe organ and would listen in awe to the rich sounds, and wonder how the organist managed to play that wonderful music with both hands and both feet. It became a dream of mine, which I ultimately fulfilled. When I went to university, I completed the Associate Diploma in piano performance. I also had lessons on the college organ.

I learnt to play with both hands and both feet. I was able to produce those beautiful sounds, which I had loved listening to as a child. I loved it!

More than anything else, Sunday school, and later youth fellowship and church drew me into a deep relationship with God. As a child, and even as a teenager, I cried every Good Friday. I felt the separation and the sadness of Jesus dying on the cross, and on Easter Sunday, I would rejoice again

Though the Storms Rage
Yet Will I Dance

My relationship with God carried me through my childhood and teenage years when deep personal relationships were missing. He is still an abiding, daily presence and help in my life.

While it appeared outwardly that there was a good relationship between my stepmother and myself, it was far from the truth. My stepmother had two personas. One she would show to the world. The other was reserved for me. Time and time again, a similar scenario would be acted out.

'You're useless. You'll never amount to anything. You're only fit for the garbage tip!' she'd yell at me. My shoulders would drop, and I'd end up in tears. I felt crushed and very alone. If something is verbally hurled at you often enough, you begin to believe it. It changes you.

When an impossible situation presents itself, you have two options, fight or flight. Most of the time I chose to flee from the situation, to hide. Flight became my main coping mechanism throughout my life. Eventually I learnt other ways to cope, but as a child, it was easier to just run away or withdraw into my own world.

As a teenager, I would often become angry and shout back, before the inevitable tears came. Then somebody would knock on the door and this absolute dragon of a woman would change instantly into this loving, sweet, charming and often hard-done-by woman. However, I could not change my mood, my tears, my dejection or my anger. A story would be spun, and I would be portrayed as this terrible child who could and would do nothing right. What could I, a child, do against this horrible insidious, unjust, two-faced behaviour? In truth, I was shackled.

I remember one instance when my stepmother was being especially nasty. I had been helping a man by playing the accompaniments for him while he sang. We were preparing a tape to be sent to his friends in Malawi, Africa. When he came to the door one particular day, my stepmum was all smiles, sweet and charming. I, however, was a mess. My eyes were red and swollen, my nose was red and I could not switch to

Chapter 1 – Finding Me
Cinderella Reworked

another persona. I tried to bluff my way out of it. 'I've been peeling onions.' He looked at me and saw through to the truth of the situation. I don't know how I did it, but I pulled myself together, sat at the piano and played while he sang. We recorded the session, and the tape was posted to Malawi.

Did I feel good about it? No. Did I accomplish what had to be done? Yes. How did I do it? I don't know.

I guess duty kicked in, aided by a sweet gentle man. Love of music and the act of making music helped me to forget the abuse temporarily and to connect with what I loved and was good at.

There was one person who saw through my stepmother. Maybe he knew the truth. I don't know. I don't think laws against child abuse were in place back in the 1950s and 1960s. As a teacher, I am now duty bound to report to the authorities if I know or suspect a child/teenager is being abused in any form.

My doctor, Dr. Mooy, knew that I was desperately unhappy. He would see me in the surgery and always made a follow-up appointment. He barred my stepmother from accompanying me into his surgery. It was always just him and me. During these appointments, he would encourage me to talk and to draw on my own inner strengths, to not let go of who I was. I remember once telling him about an incident in a book, which my sister had sent for my birthday. (I always received the books, but never the cards or letters. My stepmother destroyed those.) In the story, the young girl's mother was involved in a car accident outside their home, and in desperation, the girl was able to wrench open the jammed door to reach her mother. My doctor said, 'Marion, just like that young girl in the book, you also have reserves of inner strength that you can draw on. Never give up.'

Well Dr Mooy, wherever you are, I'd really like you to know I didn't give up and that I succeeded in life. Thank you.

Though the Storms Rage
Yet Will I Dance

As well as those special people who helped me grow and got me through the tough times, there were also many places of refuge to which I escaped. One of these places was the world of music.

An ancient, honky-tonk piano resided in our old farmhouse. Whenever I could, I would sit at the piano and pick out different tunes. I asked if I could learn but the answer was always no. I didn't know why, but I guess looking back now and knowing Dad's life, it brought back too many painful memories. Dad's banjo-mandolin sat on top of the piano, along with several old community song books. After a long, hard day's work, Dad would often get his mandolin and play. I taught myself to read the music, and could soon play *Juanita*, *The Yellow Rose of Texas*, and other songs. Also on the piano was an old *'Sankeys' Hymn Book*. It wasn't long before I could play several of those old hymns. When I was eleven, Dad finally agreed for me to have lessons.

My teacher, Heather, was only about seventeen. She was beautiful with long wavy brown hair. I remember her wearing bright, colourful sundresses and she would often bring bunches of sweet peas into the studio in springtime.

I loved playing the piano, and it became my lifesaver. When life was too hard, I could bury myself in my music. A dream was born. I would be just like my wonderful piano teacher. I too would teach piano and I would fill my life with music, light, fragrance - with all things beautiful. Heather provided for me a tangible expression of a dream, of a goal, which I steadfastly set my sights on. She gave me a very special place, filled with music and beauty. She provided an escape from the prison in which I found myself.

I became that piano teacher, a classroom music teacher, an examiner, a composer and a recording artist. It is far more than my original dream, which began its fulfilment with my first lesson at the piano with Heather.

Chapter 1 – Finding Me
Cinderella Reworked

While the house was the place I ran from, the farm was the place I escaped to. The farm was my refuge. Had Dad bought only a house, my life would have been very much harder. How I loved the farm. When we lived there, it was a poultry farm/market garden. The house was at the top of the hill, flanked on either side by other houses. The farm spread out down the hill, across the river flats and branched out behind the houses on either side of our house. The bore was at the top of the hill with a high elevated tank beside it. The tank stand was covered with thick vines bearing yellow flowers in season. Shelves were built under the tank. Cooled by the tank and the thick foliage of the vines, they provided a cool larder for the bottled fruit and vegetables, jams, pickles and relishes which my stepmother made. Pumpkins, onions and potatoes were also stored there, along with honey from our beehives. The sloped land was divided into poultry yards. Each yard had a shed containing laying boxes for the chooks to lay their eggs in, roosts to sleep on, and feed and water troughs.

Over the years our small farm had been a vineyard, a nursery, an orchard and a dairy. Each of these ventures had left its footprint on the property. Many of the citrus trees still bore fruit—oranges, mandarins, tangerines, grapefruit, lemons and limes.

Rows of grapevines yielded abundant crops each year, albeit the lower fruit was always absent thanks to my dog Scamp and the chooks making sure they got their share.

When the apricots were ripe, Scamp and our white and caramel-coloured, Guernsey milking cow would join forces for a seasonal picnic. Socks would reach for the lowest branches and shake them until the fruit fell, then they would feast on the harvest.

A road ran down the middle of our farm, from the top of the hill down to the river flats. Flanking the road on the right as we descended the hill, were the terraced garden beds. A rustic log bridge spanned the dry creek bed, playing host to an old rambling rose, which still flowered, providing colour and fragrance. Down on the river flat were the lucerne paddocks, the market garden, and the working well. Fig trees spread their branches over the remains of two other wells. The barn held our dry hay, tractor, trailer and various farm implements. At the back of the barn was an old wine cellar, partly built into the side of the hill. On the slope to the right was the orchard. On the river flat, the long paddock extended from the foot of the hill to the riverbank. The cow bale nestled at the foot of the hill near the orchard.

I am sure my love of gardening grew from the years I spent down on the farm. When I am stressed, getting into the garden is my release valve. I'm sure it was thus, even when I was a child.

I remember one chore I had to do, which for me was pure exhilaration. We grew our own lucerne and dried it to provide hay for our animals. Dad would cut it with our tractor and then we would rake the lucerne into rows, leaving it to dry in the sun. After a couple of days, we would turn the hay with a long turning fork so that the other side would dry.

We would then repeat this turning until the hay was totally dry. If it was damp and the hay was stacked, heat would build up inside the hay until it would ignite and we could lose all our hay, the barn and machinery.

If the hay was dry and ready to be taken into the barn and a summer afternoon storm threatened, we had to act quickly to get it into the barn. Dad also did bricklaying, and if he was not home, and I was back from school before the storm broke, then the task fell to me to get as much of the hay in before the first drops fell. I would hook up the trailer to the tractor, grab a pitchfork and head out into the paddock. As the gathering clouds thickened and darkened, and the thunder rumbled and built in intensity, I would throw the hay onto the trailer. When the trailer was full, I would drive it into the barn and unload it. Then back into the paddock I would go. The wind would pick up and it would be me with my pitchfork, tractor and trailer against the elements. It was wild. It became a dance between me and the approaching storm. It was a competition. Sometimes I won. Sometimes the storm won and the lucerne would need to dry out

Chapter 1 – Finding Me
Cinderella Reworked

again. Whichever way it turned out, the excitement of the dance against the approaching storm became a very special memory.

The lucerne paddock was an easy place to escape to. I would run into the paddock and then carefully pick my way into the centre of a field of full-grown lucerne where no one could see me. I would lie on my back staring up into the sky. Clouds passing over became characters in stories that I made up.

I talked silently to God in the midst of the field and He met me there. Some of my most precious times with the Lord, my Help, were in the lucerne paddock.

In the summer, the willow trees were dressed in thick green dresses. The foliage was so thick that they formed rooms. Often, I sat in amongst the willows, while the gurgling song of the river calmed me.

Bordering the farm was a lane planted with huge, ancient, mock orange trees, so big that they interlocked branches. In season, these trees bore large, green/yellow knobbly fruit. Although looking like large wild oranges or grapefruit, they were inedible. Beneath these trees was a soft lush carpet of clover. I didn't use this spot often because it was also a favourite haunt of snakes, but on the occasions that I did, I would search for four-leaf clovers and was always able to find one or two.

In cold wet weather, the hay in the barn was where I would hide. My cat, Mittens, would invariably curl up in the hay beside me.

I loved the barn with its collection of farm implements and the sweet fragrance of the hay. There could be an emotional storm up in the house, pelting rain drumming a tattoo on the tin roof of the barn or a wild storm raging outside, yet I felt safe in the warmth of the hay with Mittens curled up and purring beside me.

I loved the solitude of all these places, my refuges, where I had space to unwind, to process the turmoil in my life, to talk to God and to dream big dreams

Though the Storms Rage
Yet Will I Dance

My stepmother had a beautiful garden, but she let me know, the garden was her domain. I was not allowed any flowers from her garden. That was okay. I was still able to see the beautiful flowers and smell their fragrance as it wafted on the breeze and hung in the hot summer air.

Even as a child I wanted to make posies, bouquets, wreaths and garlands. The farm had an abundance of flowers and shrubbery. The vine with its yellow flowers growing on the tank stand became the base for wreaths and garlands. Wildflowers, including the yellow dandelions and white clover, would be gathered to make posies. Garlands for my hair included roses from the old log bridge, grape vine tendrils, lemon blossoms and various fruit blossoms. I used autumn leaves, rose hips and dry grasses. The flax, a long-leafed plant which grew by the well would be cut and stripped into thin strong ribbons which I used to bind my creations together. An old disused chook pen became my cubby house, and I would decorate it with my floral creations. In adulthood, I did a two-year TAFE course in floristry. My love of floral design was founded during my childhood on the farm.

In springtime, the orchard was my favourite place to be. The tall almond tree with its white blossoms, I imagined to be a bride. The apricot, peach, nectarine and plum trees, in their varying shades of pink, were the bridesmaids and fallen petals were the confetti. Long after I had left the farm, I chose the colours of the orchard for my own wedding dress and those of my bridesmaids and flower girls.

When I was sixteen, my parents went away on a trip and I lived for a while with Mr and Mrs Silva and their three foster children. It was there that I experienced what a real, loving family felt like. While my stepmother had a wardrobe overflowing with lovely new clothes and shoes, I had very little.

One day Mrs. Silva asked me, 'Marion, if you bought a new dress, what would you buy?'

Chapter 1 – Finding Me
Cinderella Reworked

I knew what my dream dress at that time would be, so the answer was immediate. 'A lemon lace dress.'

She made it for me, a lemon lace dress lined with satin in a fitted princess-style, falling softly from the bodice with a boat-neckline and short fitted-sleeves. I still had that dress twenty years later. It was made with love, and I cherished it. Another girl at church wore embroidered linen shifts, and I must have commented on how beautiful they were. Mrs. Silva took me shopping and we came home with a sky-blue scalloped and embroidered length of linen, and another length of white linen, embroidered with pink flowers. I then had three beautiful dresses, made for me by a woman who knew how to love and care for the unloved.

My parents completed their trip and I returned home. My stepmother became even more abusive. When home was intolerable, I would often go to the adjoining farm where Mrs Pank lived with her son, Bob. He was twenty years older than me and managed the farm while his mum took care of the house and garden.

Mrs. Pank was crippled from a fall she had suffered many years before when trying to carry two full buckets of water from a well. Her husband had left for greener pastures, leaving her to bring up her children, crippled and alone. This beautiful, gentle lady maintained a sweet positive nature. She never displayed bitterness. Shortly before moving to the farm next to ours, she had lost her only daughter to hepatitis. Mrs Pank was grieving for her daughter and I was desperate for the love of a mother. It seemed as though we had been put in each other's lives to help meet those deep needs.

Despite her handicap, this lady's house and garden were immaculate. A lovely polished wood trolley with two trays enabled her to move throughout the house, cleaning, polishing her furniture, cooking wholesome farm-fresh meals and keeping the cookie jars full of homemade biscuits – Monte Carlos, jam drops, Anzac biscuits and more. At the foot of the steps stood another trolley. She kept a rug and small hand-held gardening tools on this trolley and her bountiful and colourful

Though the Storms Rage
Yet Will I Dance

herb and flower garden was maintained beautifully. Bob did the heavy work which she couldn't manage. Bob was gentle, dependable and trustworthy. He became the big brother I didn't have.

The day finally came when I could take no more abuse. I ran down the road of our farm, climbed through the fence and made my way up the hill to Mrs Pank's and Bob's home. Bob went with me to collect all of my belongings. We loaded it into his utility and took it all back to his mum. When Dad returned home from work, he came down to the Pank's home.

Bob stood beside me. Mrs Pank looked at me and then turned to Dad.

'Marion 's home is now with us. Go home and leave her alone. She is in our care.'

From that day on, Mrs Pank was my mother and Bob was my big brother and protector. There are two rituals I learned while living with Mrs Pank and Bob that I still enjoy now; my love of scrambled eggs with last night's potato chopped into it; and tea and bikkies, first thing in the morning and last thing at night.

I have very special memories of arranging flowers from Mrs Pank's garden, in a shallow, green-glass, fluted bowl with a statue of a beautiful young girl standing in the centre of it.

My fondest memory of Bob was during a period of time when I had a stalker. It was August. I had a studio in town, above Paling's Music Store on Brisbane St. Tamworth. The eisteddfod was in progress and I had students competing. It was held in the Town Hall, a block away. A young, dark-haired man would watch me and when I left my studio to walk to the eisteddfod, he would follow me.

Each night when I finished teaching for the day and was ready to go home, he would be waiting. I was the last person to leave. I needed to walk down the street to the taxi rank, two blocks away.

Chapter 1 – Finding Me
Cinderella Reworked

If the stalker chose to come up the stairs, after my last student had left, I had no escape. I went home and poured out my fears to Mrs Pank and Bob.

'I'm scared! He is always watching me, and he follows me.' From then on, there was no need to fear. Bob would come downtown to my studio, knock on my door and call out, 'It's Bob,' and he would take me home. I later learnt that the police were watching my stalker. Soon after, he was extradited as an illegal immigrant.

Now I had a family who loved me, cared for me and really did protect me when I needed it.

The Next Ten Years

I have dwelt largely on periods and events in my life which were difficult. Not all my life, however, is marked by struggle, pain and emotional turmoil. When I turned twenty, I entered a springtime season of life when soft gentle breezes blew on me as I experienced and embraced many new and exciting events.

I entered college in 1968, graduating in 1971 with a Diploma of Secondary Teaching, (music and home science) and the Associate Diploma of Piano Performance.

After graduating, I moved back to Tamworth where I quickly established a successful piano studio. I moved into a lovely, small, self-contained flat with my newly acquired kitten, Trixie. She was a small bundle of ginger and white fur who accompanied me almost everywhere. She would lie under the organ stool when I practised at my church. While driving, she would lay along the back window of my car and observe the world passing by. When my friends and I went swimming in a creek just out of town, Trixie would be paddling away beside me.

I tried to get a teacher who would tutor me for the TMusA, a licentiate teaching diploma in pianoforte, offered by the Australian Music Examinations Board (AMEB). Unable to get a teacher, I read the requirements and set out to fulfill them.

The eisteddfod was in session. The adjudicator for that year was Nancy Salas, an excellent piano teacher from the Sydney Conservatorium of Music. The AMEB secretary for Tamworth, knowing what I was trying to achieve, arranged for me to meet with Nancy at the conclusion of the eisteddfod. In a two-hour session, Nancy guided me through the requirements, telling me what books to purchase, and how to approach each section of the exam which consisted of a three-hour written exam and a practical exam combining performance and teaching.

Though the Storms Rage
Yet Will I Dance

I sat the written exam in September 1972 at Tamworth, then in November flew to Sydney where I sat the practical examination at the Sydney Conservatorium. The pass rate for students sitting for the TMusA that year was 20% but with the guidance from Nancy, sheer determination and lots of hard work, I was successful. I was one of the 20%. I now had my third music teaching qualification.

In December 1973, two of my senior students and I, loaded my little car with our suitcases and headed south to Newcastle. We had booked into a music seminar for a week. During that week three young men, attending a church camp nearby, were praying between meetings that God would lead each of them to the woman who would be his soulmate. My future husband, Kola was one of those three men. We met that week and in October the following year, we married. By the end of that year, all three men were married.

Timmy, our first child was born in June 1975. He was tiny, and being born prematurely, he spent the first two weeks of his life in a humidicrib.

We lived in a large caravan which we had bought from friends. Our caravan was located at the very end of a valley where the two mountain ranges met each other. The first two years of our marriage was spent at this idyllic spot. I had a few piano students to teach, but mostly I threw myself into being a stay-at-home wife and mother. We ground our own flour and I baked bread, biscuits and cakes. I made vegetarian savouries and grew fresh vegetables.

From my kitchen table I could watch turtles swimming in the dam and observe a small green tree-snake sunbake daily on the old wooden gate. Kangaroos grazed on the lush pasture and possums tried to get into my van through the skylight each time I baked. Wonga pigeons, along with other birds came daily for handouts. We may have just been in a caravan, but we owned it, so were not losing money in rent.

Chapter 1 – Finding Me
The Next Ten Years

When Timmy was 16 months old, we sold the caravan, bought an old red truck with canvas sides and top and no doors. We loaded all our earthly possessions into our truck, rugged up like eskimos and set off for Tasmania, where we had bought, sight-unseen, (due to airstrikes and foolhardiness), an old timber house on three and a half acres of land. It was situated at Strathblane, just six kilometres north of the southern tip of Tasmania. I was five months pregnant.

Arriving at our 'house', we looked with horror at the walls which rose and fell like the waves on the sea. We looked at each other and cried. Then we toughened up, and with the help of friends, re-stumped and renovated our 'house' making it into our home. Life was very good

Reflection questions for Personal or Group Discussion

Though the Storms Rage Yet Will I Dance speaks of many very painful situations. These include death of a child, spouse, parents and best friends; the effect of lies and abuse on my life; and a quest to find my true identity. It deals with being displaced, loss of self-worth, isolation and attempted suicide.

In order for healing to come for deep issues we need to be willing to be vulnerable. We need to be willing to face the pain and walk through it. Sometimes we need to revisit areas of deep pain, which have been locked away in the recesses of our hearts for years. It is not easy.

Recently I had a dream, which I knew would become part of the preface to the questions in my book.

I dreamt I was in a large cave. Running through the cave was a stream of deep turbulent water. This water entered a dark tunnel. I was afraid of the deep water. I was afraid of the turbulence, and I was afraid of the confined space of that tunnel.

Others in the cave had already jumped in and were calling me to jump. Fear gripped me. I recoiled and stepped back.

'I can't!' Then a man stepped forward and wrapped his arms around me, locking his wrists together in a safe, secure grip.

He told me to do likewise, so I did. I knew, even in the dream, that this was my Lord. As he held me, we jumped together into the deep, dark turbulence.

A week later, I needed that dream so very much. My little sixteen-year-old dog, Cinders was going into a rapid decline, as her liver was no longer functioning. I knew I had to say goodbye. Penny, a friend who is a

Though the Storms Rage
Yet Will I Dance

vet, came to my home. As I held Cinders in my lap, Penny put her to sleep. Everything in me screamed, 'No, I can't', but at the same time I called on Jesus to embrace me and we jumped together. He held me. He is still holding me.

So it is, when we need to revisit those past, painful episodes in our lives, in order to receive healing. We cry out, 'I can't!', but if you ask Him, Jesus will be with you and He will not let you go.

Are you in a place of trust with someone—relative, friend, teacher or other- where you feel safe enough to allow yourself to be vulnerable, and to speak of the abandonment, abuse, feeling of inferiority, deep loss or any other painful experience from which you need release? I have provided a set of reflection questions for each chapter. You may find these helpful in working through these issues. God strengthen and comfort you as you journey and learn to dance in the rain.

Chapter 1 Finding Me ~ For Reflection

1. Do you know who you are? For me, I needed to find out who my mother really was. From that knowledge came an understanding of who I am and what I am. For you, it could be some other part of you that is hidden and needs to be unearthed.

2. Do you, or someone you know, feel abandoned in anyway?

3. Have you had lies spoken about you that hurt or hindered you in becoming the person you were born to be? Renounce those lies and the hold they have over you, in the name of Jesus.

4. Are you struggling with low self-esteem? Do you feel you are not worthy of anything, useless, not good enough, or ugly? Do you have any other negative beliefs or feelings about yourself? Ask Jesus how He sees you.

5. Do you have a safe refuge to go to when life is tough? Think of a person you trust or a place either in or out of your home where you could go.

6. Do you need to forgive anyone? Are you holding bitterness because of what has happened to you? Ask God to help you to truly forgive and be able to move on in freedom.

Chapter 2 – Tabitha

1. Tabitha
2. Learning to Dance
3. Reality
4. Compassionate Friends
5. Wet Rain
6. Out of the Ashes
7. Luke
8. Marigolds to Magnolias
9. Something More

Tabitha

I have heard said, or seen written so many times, the sentiment – 'They have great faith', or 'their faith has been rewarded', when prayer has been answered and their precious loved one has been restored to health.

But what about the enduring faith of those whose prayers seemingly have not been answered? What about those people? What happens when healing has not come and they live out their lives caring for their unhealed loved one, or stand at the grave of their loved one, with their hopes, their dreams and their aspirations lying in a fallen heap at their feet?

The saying, *'Life isn't about waiting for the storm to pass; it's about learning to dance in the rain'*, has no greater meaning, nor a greater challenge, than in such a situation.

On February 13, 1977, our precious daughter Tabitha was born. She weighed seven and a half pounds, with a thick mop of dark brown hair, ten fingers, ten toes and appearing perfect in all aspects. She was our much loved and wanted daughter, and a sister to our first born, our dear twenty-month-old Timmy who promptly renamed her Taba because he could not get his little tongue around her full name

I spent a week in hospital after Taba's birth. It didn't take long to discover that something was not as it should be. When I put her to my breast to suckle, she would take about two mouthfuls, then pull back and begin panting as though trying to get her breath. When I took my concern to the doctor, he looked at me, tapped me on the shoulder and replied,

'She's a perfectly healthy baby. You're just a panicky young Mum.'

I turned away from him, fists clenched under the bedcover and said nothing, but internally I screamed at him, 'How dare you patronise me. I'm not a first-time mum, I've breastfed Timmy for thirteen months, I'm a member of the Nursing Mothers Association, and I **know** that Tabitha's feeding pattern is **not** normal.'

We took Taba home and became a family of four. Six weeks later I returned to the doctor for the post-natal check-up. Again, I broached my concern and again I received the same demeaning answer.

Thankfully, in Tasmania at that time, I had a visiting nurse who did home visits for all newborn babies. We came under the care of Jennifer, a totally capable and experienced baby-care nurse, whose husband was a doctor. She agreed with me that something was wrong. Jennifer made an appointment for me to see her husband, who then transferred us to a specialist. Taba was booked in to the Royal Hobart Hospital, where extensive tests were carried out. The diagnosis given was congenital heart deformity. The prognosis was death at an early age. We were devastated, but we went home and determined to give our children as happy and as normal a life as we could give them.

The medical team from Hobart Hospital sent Taba's data to The Princess Alexandra Children's' Hospital at Camperdown, Sydney, New South Wales. In due course, we received a letter from a person giving us a date in February of the new year for surgery. The letter informed us they could operate, that she would only need one operation and that Taba would have a 98% chance of living a normal life. Kola and I hugged each other and our children as hope took the place of despair in our hearts.

Meanwhile Kola had applied for, and obtained, a position as an accountant/auditor at Tamworth, Northern New South Wales. We packed all our belongings onto a large trailer and Kola drove to Tamworth, a distance of 2092 kilometres. The hospital arranged flights for Timmy, Taba and me because they didn't think she would survive the long road trip with her heart condition. By now Timmy was three years old, Taba was twenty-one months old and I was eight months pregnant with our third child.

Chapter 2 – Tabitha
Tabitha

I breastfed Taba for thirteen months, in an effort to build up her immunity. It worked, for in her short life, she never had a cold or any other illness, apart from her heart condition.

Timmy and Taba were inseparable. I would put them to bed, Timmy in his bed and Taba in her cot, only to check on them later and find both of them asleep in her cot. Sometimes Timmy would open the cot, and they would both creep out as quiet as mice into the hall, just short of the dining room, where Kola and I would be. We'd find them asleep side by side on the cool linoleum of the hall floor.

Once, when I had just completed all the housework, including the washing and ironing, I went outside to check on them. It had rained earlier in the day, and I found the pair of them sitting in a very muddy puddle having a wonderful time. I hurried back inside for my camera. I still have that precious photo.

There was a creek not far from where we lived. When the water level was fairly low, the water flowed through a big pipe below the surface of the causeway. When the creek was at this level, it was safe for the children. My two little water babies would laugh and shriek with joy as the water carried them through the pipe and bounced them over smooth rocks, into the shallow pool at the base where their Dad would catch them.

Taba embraced life with enthusiasm, showing almost no fear of anything. The only thing she was afraid of was thunderstorms. She was on daily medication to slow her heart rate and it was stabilising her very well, except during a thunderstorm. To settle her, we would pick her up, hold her and seek to distract her from the storm in an effort to keep her heart beating at an acceptable rate.

One month after moving from Tasmania, Jonathon was born, weighing eight pounds. He was strong and healthy.

The next two months passed quickly. It was summer. We went for walks in the cool evenings, and spent many hours frolicking in the nearby creek. To an onlooker we seemed to be a happy and carefree family, but the clock was ticking.

Although the promised future looked bright, there was still a small element of risk, bringing with it a certain amount of apprehension.

The morning before the surgery we sat around the table ready to have breakfast. When we asked who wanted to pray a blessing, Taba was first to respond. We bowed our heads as she prayed in her nearly two-year old voice,

'Dear Jesus, tank you for dis food. Amen'

My best friend Joan from Huonville, Tasmania had arranged for a corporate prayer meeting for Taba's wellbeing during a church camp meeting, which was being held at the same time that we were in the hospital.

Standing by her bed, we listened as the surgeon spoke, 'We have decided to bring the operation forward twenty-four hours. We will operate today.'

Breakfast was brought around, but Taba was now nil by mouth – she saw a banana and cried 'nana nana', but we could not give it to her. Soon she was wheeled into surgery. They were the last words she spoke. She died the next morning without regaining consciousness.

Because she died less than twenty-four hours after surgery, it became necessary for an inquest and an autopsy (undertaken by a different hospital). Police were summoned and we were taken to her and asked to identify her.

The surgeon who operated spoke to us and cried with us. He too was a father, and it was never his intent for her to die.

After Taba died, we returned again to our room to collect our belongings.

Chapter 2 – Tabitha
Tabitha

A woman who had just lost her only child, turned on me, railing at me, 'It's alright for you, you've got two more'.

It shook and shocked me. Yes, her path was the harder path, but it no way negated my grief. I had just lost Taba and no other child could ever replace her. She was unique, as is every living person. My grief for my child was also overwhelming. I felt for that woman, but I also felt my own grief.

Another woman also approached me, just after Taba died. 'Your daughter died because you had no faith'.

That was a false and extremely cruel thing to say, trying to load condemnation and guilt onto someone who was already burdened with grief. I guess my way of dancing in those instances was to give love and forgiveness in return, however hard that was for me to do.

By the time of the prayer meeting, which was to have been held, she was gone. The church in Tasmania banded together and paid for Joan's airfare so that she could come to us.

The funeral was one week later, one day before what would have been her second birthday.

We had a graveside service, taken by one of Kola's best friends, Warren. We chose to walk to the cemetery, which was only a short distance from where we were staying. We were met by friends at the cemetery gates. Flanked by them, we walked the remaining few steps to the graveside. Surrounded by friends and relatives, we said goodbye.

Later, that afternoon, we returned to the cemetery with Joan and our boys. Timmy chose a plastic yellow and white wreath from amongst the many tributes and we let him take it home as a final gift from his sister.

We had inscribed on her epitaph:

"Goodnight Darling

See You in the Morning"

Learning to Dance

A week prior to Taba's death, Kola had declared, 'If she dies, I'll have nothing more to do with God'.

Now, only a day after her death he spoke again, his deep grief-stricken eyes boring into me. 'I have to return to college, complete my theology degree and go into ministry.' I nodded my agreement and mentally began packing for yet another move, four hours south to a bible college near Newcastle. Another change and more upheaval.

Joan travelled with us on our return to Tamworth and helped me pack up Tabitha's clothes. We then continued to pack everything else. Kola and I went together to Kola's workplace, where he put in his resignation. That weekend, Kola preached in church. I struggled to maintain my composure, so rose from my seat and walked outside. One of the men followed me and gave me a glass of water. He didn't know what to do to help me, but he felt he needed to do something. It was only a glass of water, proffered as a gift, a token of his concern, but to me it was as though he was giving me the best wine in a golden goblet.

The next day I went with Joan to book her flight home. The attendant beamed at us, 'Beautiful Day!' I muttered an affirmative, but internally I was angry that the sun had risen. How dare the sun rise and life go on as normal. Life for me was no longer 'normal' and I couldn't imagine that it ever would be again.

People showered us with flowers, food, love and attention. Even as Kola, Timmy and I struggled with our new normal, I soon learnt that we weren't the only ones coming to grips with our situation.

One day, when walking along the main street of town, I saw a friend walking towards me. She looked up, recognised me, and crossed to the other side of the street. Sometime later I learnt the reason why. She didn't

Though the Storms Rage
Yet Will I Dance

know what to say to me, so took evasive action. In that moment of time, neither of us knew the steps of this strange new dance of grief.

***

Within two weeks of Taba's death, we had relocated to Newcastle. The college administration wanted us to live in the married student quarters. They were modern, comfortable and convenient for the students. They provided friendship and support for the women and playmates for the children. However, all I could see were shared walls, no fences, and no solitude or space where I could process my loss and care for my family my way.

A friend from our church back in Tamworth rescued us by buying a large caravan for us. It had a children's bunk bed area at one end, our bedroom at the other end and a kitchen, dining room and a shower in the central section. It also had a full-length annexe. We put our caravan at the back of a friend's house, on a farm owned by their next-door neighbour. The farmer ran cattle on the property as well as poultry sheds, which were situated much further back.

Kola secured a lot of wooden pallets from a nearby factory. We laid carpet in the annexe and put my piano, our lounge, bookcases and the washing machine inside. The annexe was fully sealed from the weather and dampness. This became our home for the next three years. I loved my caravan home. We bought a swing set and a small shed for our toilet and garden tools. Between the shed and the swings, we strung lines for the washing to dry. Kola made a frame next to the swings and made a sand pit for our boys. The farmer let us fence in a yard for ourselves and I collected many styrofoam boxes from the greengrocer. I filled them with potting mix and Timmy and I planted flowers, herbs and vegetables – lots of them.

Soon I had a beautiful flower-filled yard, vibrant with colour and fragrance. Sweet peas climbed the fence, and many different flowers added their beauty to the haven we had created. When our farmer friend, saw our garden in boxes, he told me I could plant in the ground and he provided

Chapter 2 – Tabitha
Learning to Dance

me with all the cow and poultry manure I needed. Soon I had an overflowing vegetable garden. Timmy, baby Jonathon and I would take our excess vegetables to the retirement village where we regularly sold enough to buy the rest of our grocery needs. Nearby was a food factory where I bought factory seconds. With the combination of homegrown vegetables and herbs, fresh eggs and milk from the farm, home-baked bread, savouries and spreads, we ate very well.

Over the next three years we acquired a library of books. Added to Kola's theology and Greek books, we bought several series of books for our children. Amongst these was the *Little House on The Prairie* series by Laura Ingalls Wilder.

We aligned ourselves with the pioneering spirit of the stories and it overflowed into our lifestyle. Our caravan and garden on the farm was our personal 'little house on the prairie'.

We also bought the *Looney Coon* series, a set of books based on the characters and antics of raccoons, porcupines and other wildlife who frequented the island home of Giny and Sam Campbell, in the wilds of Wisconsin, America.

We had our own special wildlife visitor during this time. Ratty, named after Ratty from *Wind in the Willows*, came regularly to the door of the caravan. Although I named him 'Ratty' he was a lovely furry bandicoot. He was very quiet and would eat very gently out of our cupped hands. We all grew to love him very much.

My sister-in-law, Margie and her two daughters used to visit regularly. One particular day, their visit coincided with an appearance by 'Ratty'. I didn't know he was there until I was shaken out of my thoughts by a blood-curdling scream. I rushed to the door and saw Margie and girls backing out of the yard, finger pointed towards 'Ratty' who was making his retreat in the opposite direction.

'There – there's a – RAT!' Another shriek, and further retreat from both parties followed.

Though the Storms Rage
Yet Will I Dance

'That's not a rat! That's Ratty our pet bandicoot.'

'A bandicoot! He looks like a rat to me!'

Sometime later, my Dad called in to see us at the same time that Ratty had come to visit. Dad picked up a spade and ran towards him.

'No. Stop! That's our pet bandicoot! We call him Ratty.'

Dad advanced a few more steps. 'That's no bandicoot.'

I stood my ground and Ratty made a safe escape.

After that Kola and I had to concede that Ratty was indeed a rat. If he was going to live a long and happy life, he would need to be rehoused. We caught him, put him in a box and took him out into the bushland nearby. We all shed tears over Ratty, but it had to be.

Grief does not have a set of rules. Most of us have heard of the stages of grief, but the truth is that each individual deals with their grief according to their own personality and life experience. Thus, it was for my family. Each of us dealt with our loss in our own unique way.

Kola threw himself totally into his studies. Having been away from study for some years, he did not find it easy and needed to apply himself diligently. Greek was especially a challenge. This total absorption left little time to think and grieve, and at the time was a huge help for him. He formed friendships with fellow students and took up kayaking for physical recreation and relaxation. He loved his children, and pre-bath time story reading and storytelling continued to be part of his daily routine.

Timmy missed his little sister terribly. They had been inseparable and now there was this huge hole in his life. One day he walked up to Taba's photo on the wall, shook his fist and cried, 'That's who I want'. He was only three years old. How do you explain death to a very young child? Another day he went out to the shed and brought back the spade. 'Mummy, we've got to go and dig Taba up and bring her home.' What do you say to that? I can't remember, but we worked through it somehow.

Chapter 2 – Tabitha
Learning to Dance

He was such a lonely little boy. He helped me in the garden. We bought him a lot of Lego, books and art supplies because he loved to draw and colour in. Jonathon was only a baby, and Timmy needed a playmate. Very soon into the college year, we made friends with a couple who were both students. They had a lovely little three-year- old boy who needed a carer for several hours each day. We took Mark into our home for five days a week. Timmy now had a playmate and the deep hole in his life began to fill and the grief to fade. We had Mark for three years, till both Kola and Mark's parents graduated.

When Taba died, Timmy ceased to laugh. We so longed to hear his infectious laughter but thought we'd never hear it again. Sometime later, we decided to go to a movie night at college. A film showing the antics of a mother polar bear and her two snowy white cubs was screening. The cubs fought on the snowy hill. Every now and again one or other of the cubs would lose hold of his sibling and roll over and over down the slope.

Timmy's laugh rang out, joyous and infectious, causing all those around us to laugh with him. It was a precious moment and a huge milestone in his healing.

Jonathon was only two months old when Taba died but I believe the consequence on his life was greater than the rest of us. Shortly after he was conceived, we were told by the specialist at Royal Hobart Hospital Tasmania that Taba would die and there was nothing that could be done to save her. It was not until Hobart Hospital sent off their data to The Children's Hospital, Sydney, that we were given any hope.

I remember crying out in despair, 'I don't want this new baby. I want Taba. I can't lose her.' I would have carried that desperate cry throughout my pregnancy and imprinted it on my unborn child. When Taba died, my grief was deep and intense. Timmy vocalised his grief. Jonathon was a very placid baby, and it was very easy to care for him without giving him much attention. Only when Jonathon was thirty-five years old did he tell me that he had lived for most of his life with a feeling of rejection. Even as a young child of six or seven years old, he would study for a school exam the next day. He achieved very highly, and I believe a lot of it was due to his deep need to be wanted. He is, and from his birth was always very much wanted and loved, but tragedy and grief clouded our ability to perceive and to show love as it should have been shown.

Reality

So many things reminded me of my little girl: racks of girls' dresses in the shops, toddler groups at church, seeing other women with their little girls, and conversations taking place when groups of young mothers met together. Sometimes I would hold it together, other times I could not. I would make my retreat as quickly and as unobtrusively as I could and then become a blubbering mess in the safety of my hiding place. I avoided the girls' clothing sections in shops and stayed away from the women's groups. This helped somewhat, but life took place around me and I had to learn to move on.

My husband was studying for the ministry and I was going to be a pastor's wife. How did my brokenness, God, my beliefs and my daughter's death fit together? Was there an answer or was it just one big horrible mess? If there was an answer, I needed to find it quickly. The outcome of my search was written into a letter which I sent to all our family and friends. Here is an excerpt of that letter.

It is now six months since our little Taba died, leaving us lonely and desolate. I didn't think I would be happy or light hearted again, nor did I think I would believe in God's promises again, however I have learnt that God is faithful and is a sustainer of those who cling to him, however feeble their grasp may be. I had a lot of questions to ask, especially concerning prayer and the promises of God. I finally came to the conclusion that we have reversed the correct order of things in God's overall plan.

God created Adam and Eve perfect and set them in a perfect world – a world where pain, death, suffering and loneliness had no part, and men were companions of God in a love and joy filled world. This was reality. Because God is intelligent, he gave us an intellect, because God is emotional, He gave us emotions, because God gives freely of himself to us and wants us *in turn to give freely to Him. He gave us a free will. Unfortunately for all mankind, man used his free will wrongly and thus ushered in the world we now live in – corrupt and full of misery. To me, this world while we must live in it, it is <u>unreal</u>! It is not in harmony with God's nature and was never intended for man. It is <u>unreality</u>. There are promises of God as yet unfulfilled. Thousands have languished in prisons or died a martyr's death or had trials for which there seems no apparent answer and yet looking at the lives of these people, their lives and deaths have been victorious with an overriding joy and hope. Why? Again, I believe it was for them, that this life was not reality. Reality for them was and is in the blessed hope, the fulfilment of God's promises and the ultimate answers to all our prayers. In the ordering in of a world renewed and of Eden restored, when Christ returns to claim His own, to expel Satan and sin and to continue Eden. This is again reality. Thus, it is for me. Once I came to this understanding the wound began to heal.*

I had worked through some of the questions with God, but the grief would still rise up when I least expected it. Life continued despite our loss and I found that many factors contributed to our healing.

Compassionate Friends

The three years at college were not always a progressive, upward journey from brokenness to wholeness. I counted progress in managing to get through one day without crying, then two days, then three days. I counted getting through a week as being a gigantic step, but it took me the best part of three years to get there.

Because I had completed my education and music qualifications at the same college, prior to meeting Kola, I knew a lot of people. When old friends found out that I had lost my daughter, several people came to me for help because they too were struggling with the loss or the imminent loss of a child. I felt overwhelmed. Here I was, struggling with my own grief. How could I help others with their own journeys of loss? I didn't know, but I could not turn my back on them.

The first young mum who turned to me for help was someone I had known when I went through college. I was struggling very badly with inferiority during those years. At college, Merry was a beautiful and extremely talented girl. She played several instruments, sang and was in every way far above anything I thought I could ever be. My thinking at that time was wrong. I know that now. She never knew I felt like that during the college years. Now here she was, struggling with the possible loss of one of her daughters. Grief is a strong leveller, reaching out its fingers and touching everyone at some stage of his or her life. I embraced this mum and helped and loved as best I could.

In the meantime, my worldview and the view of myself changed. I grew up. While grief is extremely painful, good things can emerge from it. This was one of those things.

The next mum who turned to me was the wife of one of the college lecturers. Her precious little boy did not have long to live. She told me, amidst her pain and grief, 'I have put everything in place, and I am ready emotionally for when I will have to say goodbye.'

Having just laid my own daughter to rest, I knew that the divide between life and death is huge. No matter how prepared you may think you are, you are laid bare emotionally when that moment comes. I stood beside her and walked step by step through her journey.

I found an organization called 'Compassionate Friends'[1] for parents and siblings of deceased children. I attended meetings and became a telephone counsellor with them. I soon realised that everyone's journey, everyone's loss, and everyone's coping strategies were very different. The best I could do was stand next to my friends and just be there. I could say, 'It's okay to be angry. It's normal'.

Wanda lost her little boy through a tragic accident. He was only a toddler and had somehow managed to get through a 'childproof' fence. In those days bread was delivered daily to your door. The baker had pulled up outside Wanda's home and it is thought that a cat must have walked underneath his van.

Wanda's little boy crawled under the van after the cat, and the baker drove off not knowing the child was there.

Music was a large part of Wanda's life. She sang and played the piano and the guitar. Not long after the death of her child, she picked up her guitar and hurled it across the room, smashing it. I sat with her as she poured it all out, her grief, anger, guilt, frustration and feeling of being helpless. I had been there and could say, 'It's okay, you are not losing it. Anger is part of grief. Your response is normal. Let it be.' I hugged her and could truly share in her grief and her emotional turmoil.

I could be there, I could listen, I could share experiences if asked for or just stand with the parents in the hospital as they said goodbye. Sometimes no words were the best words.

Chapter 2 – Tabitha
Compassionate Friends

Sometime later, I was called to a hospital where I stood with grieving parents beside the bed of their precious daughter as she took her last breath. It was so hard because it was only four years since I had stood in the same place, saying goodbye to my own daughter.

But this time it was not about me. Nor was it the time for words. I hugged the parents, stroked their daughter's hair and grieved with them both. I stayed with them until they were ready to leave the hospital. Later, at the graveside, people were coming to them with condolences. I looked across to the grandmother. We made eye contact and we nodded to each other.

Again, no words were exchanged, and yet we had communicated a deep empathy, a sharing and an understanding.

I never sought counselling for myself but I'm glad I did for my friends, and for the strangers who became friends through the shared experience of losing a child.

Wet Rain

Only a couple of months after arriving at college, Timmy was admitted to hospital and I was forced to face my fears head on. I wrote about the experience in my journal, entitling it *Wet Rain*, and I would like to share this with you.

>Rain fell in a steady drizzle, soaking the world outside and greying the sky. I stood at the window surveying the wet world out there as I struggled with the pent-up emotions inside. Back in the children's ward, Timmy lay on his bed sleeping peacefully, a patch over one eye, his blonde hair against the pillow. He was only three and a half years old. It was a simple accident, a game with a bath towel and his dad, which went wrong when a tassel from the towel flicked around his body and damaged the cornea of his eye.

>Yesterday had been all right, I was staying in the hospital with my son, comforting and reassuring him. Yesterday children had been admitted and some children had gone home and the normal routine of hospital life continued. But, today! Today was different. Today was operating day. Timmy didn't require surgery thankfully, but each time a child was wheeled out I caught my breath, the panic rising in me till I wanted to scream, till I wanted to gather my child in my arms and run from the place. But I couldn't, I was trapped.

>'Doctor Alexis will be here at about 11 am. He will talk to you when he examines Timmy,' said the nurse, as she checked his pulse.

>'Eleven O' clock, that's three hours away,' I whispered.

>'Yes, are you alright?' the nurse looked at me with concern.

>'I can't stay in here, not while they're wheeling children out to theatre.' My voice broke, 'I can't.'

Though the Storms Rage
Yet Will I Dance

'The last time I saw my daughter alive was when they wheeled her into the operating room --- she died three months ago.'

The nurse put her arm around me, 'You can wait on the veranda, come, Timmy is fine, and he'll sleep for a while yet'.

Picking up my wallet and my book, I allowed myself to be led out of the room and onto the veranda.

'The Doctor can see you out here. I'll bring you a coffee.'

'Thankyou.' Finding a window seat, I sank down onto it. Time passed slowly. Every now and then I returned to the ward. Timmy slept peacefully on but each time, another bed was vacant, and each time the grief and the panic caught in my throat threatening to overwhelm me.

Hearing the soft tread of footsteps behind me, I turned to see the doctor approaching me.

He greeted me, and opening his file began discussing Timmy's treatment. 'We'll keep him heavily sedated all week, and apply a dressing to his eye. As long as he stays still there will be no problem.'

I nodded in agreement and smiled weakly. 'I'm glad it's raining.'

Doctor Alexis looked at me. He knew why I was on the veranda. The nurse had told him. Probably wondering at my comment, he queried, 'Why?'

'My husband is very busy, and he'll probably forget to water my garden. Now I don't have to worry.'

Smiling he answered, 'I must admit, if it were me, I'd probably forget as well'.

After he left, I checked on my sleeping son once more, and walked quietly out of the ward. I resolved to go for a walk, outside, in the rain. I'd gather my thoughts and my strength for the rest of the day.

Chapter 2 – Tabitha
Wet Rain

Puddles patterned the footpath, the rain beat a steady tattoo around me and I felt the panic beginning to subside.

I sat on the bench and looked out at the falling rain.

An elderly man walked past, dragging a suitcase on wheels behind him. He looked across at me and smiled, 'Wet rain!' He commented.

'I beg your pardon?'

'Wet rain!'

'Oh, yes,' I replied, 'Yes, it is.'

The strangeness of the comment jolted me and made me think – 'wet rain', cooling, healing rain.

I stood and began walking slowly back to the hospital, occasionally lifting my hot tearstained face to the sky, letting the cool raindrops alight on my face, washing away the fear and the panic. As I walked on, my shoulders straightened and my steps quickened, till I found myself at the hospital entrance.

I smiled to myself, and knew that I could now face the day, composed and unafraid, refreshed and renewed by the soothing, wet rain.

Out of the Ashes

With shoulders slumped, Kola put the phone down and turned to me, 'Our house, it's gone, burnt to the ground.'

I stared numbly at him, unable to give a reply. I felt sick in the pit of my stomach. All that we had financially was in that house.

He shook his head, 'It's all gone, there's nothing left'.

We were now in our second year of college. The boys were growing, Kola's studies were progressing well and we were beginning to pick ourselves up from the loss of our daughter. I sank down into our lounge. Hugging each other we grappled with this new calamity.

'Why God? Wasn't losing Taba enough? Why this?'

Our old home in Tasmania sat on three and a half acres of land. We had bought it for the princely sum of $7,500. We had restumped it and put in a new kitchen with a slow combustion stove, which gave us hot water, warmth in winter and a place to dry clothes on those grey wet days. We enlarged the lounge/dining area, replaced floor coverings and painted the house inside and out. When we moved back to the mainland, we put it up for rent.

The people who moved in did not pay any rent, so we put the house up for sale. We received a buyer who offered us a figure we were happy with.

It would have covered our costs, even if it didn't make a profit. Contracts were drawn up, and we were on the point of exchange. Then came news of the fire.

A passing motorist saw the flames and ran into the place to get the people out. They were safe but had lost all of their possessions and did not have contents insurance. We had insured the place, new for old when we first bought it.

There was now, no house to buy, just a pile of ashes and rubble. The contract of sale fell through.

'Kola, we are insured, we must make a claim.' Nodding, he left me to deal with what was required. Thus, began a three-year saga.

I claimed new for old.

The insurance company replied, 'Because you no longer live in Tasmania, and you are not returning to Tasmania, you are not eligible for any claim'.

'That has nothing to do with the contract,', I said. 'My claim stands – new for old.'

The company offered a very low amount. I refused. They raised the amount slightly. I refused. Then they offered me another figure if I'd finalise within two weeks. Again, I refused.

We were matching step for step in a war dance.

Kola completed his degree and we moved to Sydney where Kola became friends with a solicitor, who took up our fight.

After some research, he found a precedent that he could use. The company had been taken to court for a very similar claim, and the claimant had won. Our solicitor then contacted the company – new for old, plus inflation, plus interest. The insurance company capitulated, and paid up all that was demanded of them.

Our war dance became an excited, jubilant victory dance.

Luke

The loss of our house by fire was only the beginning of extra hassles for that year. We had put Timmy and Jonathon to bed, and we were getting ready to climb into bed ourselves.

'Kola, I'm bleeding.' Twenty-four weeks pregnant, I should not be bleeding. Something was wrong. Getting our friends to stay with the boys, Kola bundled me into the car and drove to the emergency department of the nearest hospital.

I was admitted to hospital where I remained for ten weeks. I was diagnosed with placenta praevia. That initial haemorrhage was the first of eight, each one larger than the previous one. Soon getting up to go to the toilet or have a shower was not an option. I was confined to total bed rest.

Each haemorrhage triggered labour. I was given medication to halt the labour. The medication caused me terrible nausea and vomiting, so more medication was given, to stop me from being sick. My baby still had sixteen weeks to go, so injections were given directly into the amniotic fluid surrounding my unborn child to strengthen the lungs. I would be moved out of the ward and into a delivery room. Often Dr Fitchett, my gynaecologist would tell the staff to leave me in there for longer periods, so that Kola and I could have precious time alone.

During one of my early visits to Dr Fitchett's consulting room, we talked about Tabitha and the circumstances surrounding her death.

'You need to know the results of the autopsy and inquest. Once you know the cause of her death, then you will be better equipped to move on through the grieving process.' He made contact with the hospital where she died, to get the inquest findings.

When he checked me in hospital, he told me the inquest results had arrived and he would bring them to me.

Though the Storms Rage
Yet Will I Dance

'Just give me the letter, and leave me to read it while you go on your hospital rounds, for if you stay you know I'll fall to pieces.'

The next day, he got the nurse to draw the curtains around my bed, handed me the letter, and left to do his rounds.

I read the letter and reread it, sobbing uncontrollably as I did so. There had been a wrong diagnosis and that operation should not have been performed. Her whole heart was deformed. Instead of the one large hole which they repaired, there were also several smaller holes. The blood was being pumped from an enlarged ventricle into a ventricle which was too small to cope. Her heart could not function properly, her kidneys failed, and she died.

After completing his round, Dr Fitchett returned to me. He would have been an extremely busy man, with many demands on his time, yet he found the time to sit with me while I poured out my grief. I must have looked an absolute mess, and yet he looked past that to the hurting person that I was. Years later I learnt that he resigned from gynaecology and specialised in grief counselling.

My time in hospital would have been during his transition between leaving gynaecology and becoming a grief counsellor.

Ten weeks is a long time in hospital, especially when you are confined to bed. How was I to 'dance in the rain' while confined to a hospital bed?

'Get photos of your family and put by your bed,' my doctor suggested. But I was like my Timmy. Having photos of them nearby would just frustrate and upset me, so I chose not to have any photos. This worked for me, but I do not advocate the same for others. We must all choose what works for us.

When seventeen-month-old Jonathon woke up the morning after I was admitted to hospital and found that his mummy had deserted him, he then deserted me. For the entire ten weeks I was in hospital, he would not

Chapter 2 – Tabitha
Out of the Ashes

enter the ward, choosing instead to stand at the door and observe me from a distance. My heart broke, both for me and my little boy. I knew he was hurting but I was powerless to do anything about it. When I eventually returned home, Jonathon clung to me, like a limpet on a rock! I could not even go to the toilet without him.

Two years on, when I played the piano for church, Jono (Taba's name for Jonathon) would sit on the piano stool with me.

'Why don't you send him to the children's section?' the Senior Pastor asked me.

'If you want me to play for church, then you must accept that Jono will sit next to me. That is his choice, and I am not going to separate him from me until he is ready.'

Jono stayed safe by my side until he was secure enough to venture further afield.

Now he travels the world staying for months at a time and speaks to hundreds of people at times in his capacity as a youth missionary with Power to Change (Campus Crusade).

Friends -including students and lecturers and their wives- helped us with meals, childcare and washing, which we appreciated greatly. Even so, Kola still had his time filled with lectures, assignments and caring for the boys. Meanwhile I had time to spare. Television bored me and I needed something to do while in my bed.

The answer came in the form of Kola's assignment. Soon I had my bed covered with Greek dictionaries, lexicons and other books, paper and pens. I was no longer bored. I had a mission. I knew no Greek but with the help of the resources at hand I knew I could master this assignment. The doctors and nursing staff would come and go, as would meals, and I would be immersed in study. It opened up unbelievable conversations and I had a ball. Even Kola's Greek lecturer and his wife (who had been one of my music lecturers, years earlier) helped with food and childcare and came to visit me in hospital. Greek books were piled on my table at visiting hours and he knew that it was me who was doing the assignment, but he was okay with it. I got an A for that assignment, and I was over the moon!

As time went by, the hospital staff and I got to know each other. I became a captive listener and counsellor to many of the staff as I grew to love these precious people.

Often during a break or after their shifts, nurses or domestic staff would come, sit by my bed and pour out their lives and problems to me, and sometimes even shed tears. The patient/staff divide had come down.

I turned thirty-three while in hospital. As it was mid-week, I thought it would be a very quiet non-event. How wrong I was. The staff had organised a party for me. The kitchen staff baked and decorated a cake, complete with candles. Kitchen and domestic staff, nurses and doctors all turned up at my bedside bearing the cake, cordial and gifts to sing *Happy Birthday* and celebrate my day with me.

I remember other occasions when the staff went out of their way to do something special for me.

I was in the delivery room by myself, after a big haemorrhage and onset of labour, complicated by nausea and vomiting from the medication. I commented in passing that it would be so nice to have a cup of Bonox. The nurse I'd spoken to, busy with other mums in labour, went on a quest to find me some Bonox or Vegemite or something similar that I could drink. Sometime later she turned up with a hot cup of Vegemite, so excited that she had been able to fulfill my wish. She had handed on the request to other staff until they could find what I wanted. I drank that hot savoury drink but unfortunately was unable to keep it down for very long. Still, the thought and actions of that nurse and other staff will live forever.

With still six weeks to go to full term, and after a really big haemorrhage, Dr Fitchett came to me and told me that my baby would be born by caesarean section at 9:00 am the next morning, August 22 1980. Little Luke was born, a healthy but small, five-pound baby. He was placed

Chapter 2 – Tabitha
Out of the Ashes

immediately into a humidicrib. Sometime later when I was being taken back to the ward, a nurse brought my baby to me so that I could see and touch him. This tiny baby was wrapped in bubble wrap to keep him warm. My very precious bubble-wrap baby. Because of the injections given to him over the previous ten weeks, little Luke's lungs were strong and healthy. He remained in the humidicrib for only four hours before being placed in an ordinary crib.

Sometime after his birth, I was given a form to fill in. I had to write on that form that my daughter was deceased. Filling in that information broke me all over again. I lay under the blanket and sobbed as softly as I could. I remember it was just before visiting hour and I remained hidden under my blanket trying to stifle my sobbing. Thankfully, I had no visitors at that time. When visiting hour was over and everybody had gone, Luke was brought back into the ward, along with other babies, to be fed. As he was handed to me, I sobbed out my story to the nurse. She disappeared and shortly after, the head nurse from the nursery came to me, tucked Luke into my arms and gave me a bottle to feed him. She was so caring and gentle with me. What she did was the best possible thing she could have done.

Our babies slept in the nursery during the night, but had cribs beside our beds. Luke, however, rarely spent time in his crib. Nurses would walk past during the day and ask, 'Where is Luke?' I would lift the blanket to reveal him, sound asleep on my chest, close to my heart.

Marigolds to Magnolias

I had much to keep me occupied. I had three little boys to care for during the first year at college- my own two and our friends' son Mark. That became four little boys the second year when Luke, our third son was born. Meal preparation, housework and the garden kept my hands busy. At night, when the boys slept, I proofread and did the final copies of Kola's assignments. After Luke's birth, I needed to rebuild my physical fitness, so pulled my squash racquet out of the cupboard and joined a local club. By this time, I had also acquired several piano students. I was a music teacher and had always loved my piano. After Taba died, however, I lost my desire to play the piano and make music. My hands were busy, but my mind went too often to the place of grief.

At the beginning of our third year, my landlady knocked on my door with an advertisement for a floristry course in her hand.

'We can do it together,' Doreen pleaded while standing in my temporary garden. My garden was a blaze of happy colour, overflowing with large orange and yellow marigolds, sweet peas, pansies and daisies. A couple of weeks later, we found ourselves at the floristry course.

Florist wire? Yes.

Parafilm? Yes.

Flowers? Yes. Well, sort off!

Looking at my assortment of requirements, I gave a lopsided smile as I wondered what my floristry teacher would think of my choice of flowers.

The floristry course excited both Doreen and me. Neither one of us had much money, but we had the flowers out of my garden. The course thrilled me because it was a creative outlet and some place I could allow my thoughts to go, as I planned my next bouquet or arrangement.

Week after week, we turned up at class with our marigolds, sweet peas and daisies, while our classmates turned up with their roses, carnations and gladioli. Our tutor tore at her hair and shook her head.

' You can't make a wedding bouquet out of marigolds. The colour is wrong and they stink!'

I countered, 'Yes, the colour is wrong and they do stink, but we're learning the techniques.'

Along with fresh flowers, we learnt to use silk and dried flowers, wrapped lollies, one-dollar notes and much more. The wrapped lollies we covered with green or purple cellophane and fashioned them into bunches of grapes. Tied to a bottle of wine, they made an excellent gift for a man. One-dollar notes were fashioned into a rose.

At the end of the year, Kola graduated with his degree. We relocated to Sydney. Now we had an income. I found an advanced course in floristry and enrolled. This year was different. I could now afford to buy the correct flowers.

My wedding bouquets became magical arrangements of roses, seed pearls, gladioli and magnolias. They looked like they were meant to look.

Four years after Tabitha's death, the intense grief was gone. Two years of floristry training had given me new skills, which people were recognising. I was getting commissions for wedding flowers and for other occasions.

With the money from my first wedding bouquets, I bought a swing and gym set for my boys. I found myself back at my piano, playing for church and concerts.

Chapter 2 – Tabitha
Marigolds to Magnolias

Working on an exquisite bouquet of white magnolias, I thought of my first bouquet of pungent, bright yellow marigolds.

I had moved from crippling grief to excited anticipation of life ahead. I had moved on from marigolds to magnolias.

Something More

Our three years at college were drawing to an end. I was in the early weeks of my fifth pregnancy. The boys were all happily playing around my feet in our caravan. As I felt myself becoming increasingly dizzy, I reached for my list of telephone numbers and passed it to Timmy, who was now six years old.

'Go next door; get them to ring Aunty Daphne. Tell her to come here.' Bless him, he knew to run and do as I'd asked. I sank to the floor, fading in and out of consciousness. I had four little boys in my care, aged between six and one. Daphne came, rang for an ambulance, contacted Kola and took the boys. I was told that Timmy was hysterical when they put me in the ambulance, but he had obeyed quickly and in doing so, he saved my life.

The ambulance took me to the local medical centre where the doctor connected me to a saline drip and rang my gynaecologist. The local doctor thought I was dehydrated but Dr Fitchett, who was on holidays, told the doctor to get me to hospital immediately. In and out of consciousness I remember the blaring ambulance siren and being told they were going through traffic intersections against the lights to get me to hospital. Dr Fitchett interrupted his holiday to come to the hospital and operate.

I had an ectopic pregnancy, where the foetus had not reached the uterus and was growing in the fallopian tube. I was nine weeks pregnant when the tube burst.

The baby died and my life too was in the balance as a large quantity of my blood was flooding into my body and out of my veins. I had not lost any blood externally but the pressure inside of my body produced unbearable and incessant pain except for when I was unconscious.

Though the Storms Rage
Yet Will I Dance

Kola arrived at the hospital not long after I did. I hate to think what speeds he did to get there, but get there quickly he did, and saw me as they were wheeling me into surgery.

The anaesthetist looked at me asking, 'how much has she lost?'

'An awful lot, but it's all inside,' was the reply.

By this time my veins had collapsed, except for the lifeline inserted back at the local surgery. As the anaesthetist tried to get into a vein in my neck, the blood seeped into the surrounding tissues, causing a very large collar of deep purple bruising. The anaesthetist succeeded and Dr Fitchett operated on me, saving my life.

Later, I was told by a nurse about an incident during the surgery. Because the staff knew me from my ten weeks in hospital the previous year, I was told things which normally I would not have been told. During surgery, my heart stopped beating and I stopped breathing. A nurse was told to bring a defibrillator to the operating table. When she recognised me and realised I wasn't just a body, but a friend on the table who was dying, she panicked. The defibrillator crashed to the floor. She picked it up and although time was lost, it still worked, and the electric shock was applied which kick-started my heart into life again.

The next day, when my doctor came to see me, he told me, 'According to everything in the medical books, you should have died. You are still here because your Maker has something more for you to do'. I knew he was right, and I knew that with the passing of time God would show me what that something more would be.

Chapter 2 Tabitha ~ For Reflection

1. Are you trying to process the loss of a loved one? Or maybe you are standing by someone who is grieving. What does your new 'normal' look like? If you are a support person for someone in grief, what do you think his/her 'normal' looks like? Can you enter into it with them and learn to walk beside them?

2. How is each member of your family processing his/her grief? How can you help him/her?

3. Do you or do you have a family member or friend who feels rejected? Could it be traced back to when he or she was still in the womb?

4. There was no death in Eden, before sin changed everything and there is no death in heaven. How does death fit into our reality today?

5. Think of a time when you were talking to someone in grief. Did you have trouble knowing what to say? What seemed to help in that situation? Is there anything you would do differently? Can you think of a time when 'no words' were the best words? If you are the one grieving, what words did you find helpful? What words did you find to be unhelpful?

6. Are you a good listener, listening with compassion and no judgements, even when you don't understand? Have you tried to walk in that person's shoes and gain their perspective? What are some things which would stop you from being a good listener? What things would you change in order to be a good listener?

7. Have you asked God to walk beside you in your own grief or when walking alongside someone who is grieving? It is too hard a road to walk alone.

Chapter 3 – Displaced

1. Square Pegs
2. Changing Roles
3. On the Road
4. Descent into Despair

Square Pegs

We were country bumpkins in a high society church. Our first placement lasted one year before we moved to our second church. Kola's background was as a war refugee and I grew up on a farm. Our time in ministry after graduating lasted only four years. The four years meant four moves, four different houses and four different schools for Tim. It was a very unsettled time. We were displaced for most of this time. We soon realised that this situation was not working for us and we needed to make some changes.

We had enrolled Timmy in a church school, but that was also a big mistake. Timmy was only six years old when we entered ministry, and he had already experienced much grief and trauma. He also experienced instability from our frequent moves. The next four years compounded this instability. One day, after he had come home from school, he took me by the hand, led me out the front door and pointed behind the sweet peas, which were growing up the wall. I looked and found a watch lying on the soil. Picking it up, I looked at my small son. 'Did you steal this watch, Timmy?' He nodded. He had taken the watch off of his teacher's desk. Why did he do this? It was a cry for help.

We learnt that he would not read at school, even though we knew that he was a good reader. After searching for alternatives, we took him out of the church school and enrolled him in Rooty Hill Infants State School which had a very different approach to learning.

He had a wonderful teacher who was experienced and ran an excellent program. The change for the better in Timmy was immediate.

After two years in ministry and three house moves during that time, our next change was to buy our own house. We needed some stability in our life and owning our own home would give us that. After searching for some time, we found our home. It was a lovely three-bedroom-plus study, brick and tile home on a third of an acre block in a small satellite estate, ten minutes from Penrith, a city at the foot of the Blue Mountains. Our home already had gardens and a pool. The backyard joined and looked out onto farmland. We settled into our home and the boys settled into Luddenham State School, an old country school. The headmaster/Grade 6 teacher was very much loved, along with his Old English Sheepdog who came to school with him every day and sat in on all the lessons.

We built a chook pen along the back fence and very soon had fresh eggs from our brood. A vegetable patch yielded fresh herbs and vegetables. Binny and Kig, two loveable fluffy guinea pigs, joined our family very quickly, giving us lots of little binnykigs! A smoky dark-eyed cat we called Rumpus Galumpus also joined our family.

When I worked in the garden, Rumpus would drape himself around my neck and come along for the ride. Lassie (just like Lassie from *Lassie Come Home*) came to stay and she also provided fluffy babies.

All the boys joined the Police Citizens Youth Club (PCYC) where they all learnt judo. Tim also had art classes at PCYC and ultimately became an art/film and television teacher.

Our last two churches, which we served concurrently, were ultra conservative congregations who only wanted sermons based on the 'pillars of the faith' which outlined the church as being 'the only true church for the last days'. We however wanted to share the love of Christ and what He has done and is doing for us. This was not what these congregations wanted, and our days were numbered from the day we arrived there.

There was one part of our ministry work which we both loved very much. During our time at Cabramatta/Bankstown church, we became very involved with refugees from Laos, Vietnam and Cambodia who had managed to find their way to the refugee camps on the Thai border.

On 17 April 1975, the communist party of Kampuchea, known as the Khmer Rouge, took control of Cambodia. Their regime lasted four years until 1979 and cost approximately two million lives through the combined

Chapter 3 – Displaced
Square Pegs

results of political executions, disease, starvation and forced labour. The Khmer Rouge was eventually toppled in 1979 by Vietnam, Cambodia's neighbour and former ally. Those who survived joined thousands of refugees who fled the country, travelling huge distances on foot to reach the refugee camps on the Thai border. Cambodia became known as 'The Killing Fields'. About 100 000 men, women and children were able to make it to these camps.

Many were killed or maimed by land mines and marauding remnants of the Khmer Rouge or brutalised by the Thai military before humanitarian aid arrived.

Resettlement of these people took place, beginning in 1975 and continuing into the 1980s. Kola and I began working with these people through our church in Cabramatta, in January 1984.

Kola was born in the forced labour camp of Markt Elbracht in Germany, towards the end of World War Two and spent the first five years of his life there. In 1950 Kola, his parents and hundreds of others were taken from Germany to Naples where they were then shipped to Australia and other countries who had opened their doors to these displaced people. He spent the next five years in the migrant camp at Bonegilla on the NSW/Victorian border.

Because of his childhood experiences, Kola immediately had rapport with the Cambodian refugees arriving in Cabramatta. We spent time with many different families, drinking tea and eating rice as we listened and learnt their stories, crying with them and setting into motion actions to try and locate missing family and reunite people where we could.

One young girl, Sophanara, will forever be etched in my heart. She was twelve years old when we first met her. Forced to flee for her life, she joined a ragged band of people. Scantily clad, shoeless, still just a child, she trudged huge distances, sometimes hiding where she could from the relentless enemy.

Though the Storms Rage
Yet Will I Dance

Her parents, siblings and grandparents were all gone, slain by the Khmer Rouge. On reaching the Thai border she was taken into a refugee camp, where at last she received desperately needed help –clothing, food, clean water and medical aid from people who cared.

When she reached the camp, her name was taken and added to the lists of names which were then attached to the walls of buildings. As new arrivals flooded in, everybody – those already there and the new arrivals - daily scanned the lists, hoping against hope that they would find the name of another family member or loved one.

Another young man who had arrived sometime earlier scanned the lists as he made his painful way along the walls. One of his legs had been blown off when he stepped on a landmine. Seeing her name listed, he caught his breath. At last someone else who was family, his niece, had survived and was here in the camp with him.

This man's brother was in Australia, with his young wife and two very small children, one of them, a baby. It was at this point that we came into the picture, and worked with government authorities to reunite the remnants of their family. Sophanara was the daughter of another brother. Eventually Sophanara arrived and was taken in and cared for by her uncle and aunt. By the time we left the area in 1986, a process was in place to bring out the remaining brother. Because of his injuries it was taking longer, but he would be brought out.

The most poignant memory I have of Sophanara came from a Christmas party we gave at our church. One of the ladies, dressed as Santa Claus handed out gifts to all the children. As Santa and I moved around the hall with our big bag, we came to Sophanara's family.

The baby received a teddy bear and the little two-year-old received a doll, which she eagerly clutched to herself. Then it was Sophanara's turn. She was twelve and beautiful. We had wrapped a lovely brush and comb set in Christmas paper for her. We watched as she unwrapped it. Instead of smiles, she began sobbing. Perplexed I looked at her aunt. 'She wanted

Chapter 3 – Displaced
Square Pegs

a doll'. A doll! Quickly I despatched one of the women to our cupboard where we kept the things we had collected as gifts, and thankfully, a doll was found. Returning to Sophanara we placed the doll in her arms. She hugged the doll, gave us a watery smile and began crying again. This time however, they were tears of joy. Everyone had been watching this take place. Wiping tears from my eyes I looked around the room. People everywhere were drying their eyes. That night we all cried tears of joy for this precious child. She kept the brush and comb set for her beautiful long black hair. One of the women in our congregation was so moved by what had happened, that the next day she went to the shops, bought a beautiful doll and dressed her, especially for Sophanara.

Changing Roles

In January 1986, Kola was summoned to a meeting with the president of the organisation we were working for. It was his birthday that day. Without too many preliminaries, he was sacked from his work as a minister. We were both on holidays at the time and he was looking after our three boys while I attended a summer school. I was completing some subjects towards upgrading my teaching diploma to a Bachelor of Education degree. We were devastated. That day we didn't even have the luxury of each other's company.

We later learnt that our sacking was part of a large witch-hunt by the organization. Over a ten-year period, they sacked over a hundred and fifty theology graduates, all of whom had studied under one particular lecturer.

Looking back now, I can see God's hand over us. At the time, I am really sorry to admit, we could not. We felt lost and devastated. The world as we knew it had changed. We had gone through so many changes recently that this change seemed to be one too many.

Two years earlier, Kola had encouraged me to upgrade to my degree. The house we bought was only ten minutes' drive to the Nepean University and a little further to the Hawkesbury Campus. I completed psychology, philosophy and education subjects at Nepean and food science and technology classes at Hawkesbury. At first, I was able to attend day classes, while Kola and I juggled our times to care for our boys. When I returned to full time teaching at St Patrick's Girls School, Campbelltown in 1985, I attended night classes at university. My three boys were now all at school. In the years leading up to my returning to full-time work, I had several piano students, and taught for Technical and Further Education (TAFE) NSW on a casual basis.

Though the Storms Rage
Yet Will I Dance

Although it was a shock when Kola lost his job, we had at least two things for which we could be grateful. First, we had already paid off our house, so we didn't have any debts. Second, I had a full-time teaching position, so we had a good income.

One place I taught at was a refuge centre for abused women or men and children. Once a week, I taught budgeting, budget cooking and making patchwork cot blankets out of second-hand clothing, old blankets and whatever else we could get. At Easter, I took my chocolate-making equipment and we made baskets of eggs and filled-chocolates for the parents to give to their children. Once we had a dad at the refuge and he revelled in our Easter efforts.

I remember another day when my teaching had to be laid aside. The Federal Police came to the refuge to take three children into protective custody. Despite opposition and the wails of the children, they put them in the police car and drove away. All the staff and myself could do at the time was offer comfort to the distraught mother and try to bring peace and calm into the situation.

When we left our church, many of our congregation would ring us, asking us to come back and be with them. We could not.

We had a switch in our bedroom that we could click so that we couldn't hear the phone if it was ringing. For our own welfare, we took advantage of that switch. Every Friday afternoon we would turn the phone off and leave it off until Monday morning.

This strategy worked well until one weekend when we came unstuck. My stepmother had passed away on the Friday, and the funeral was on the Monday.

We were uncontactable. Monday morning, I took myself off to the university library to work on an assignment. I took my car, but also accidently took Kola's car keys. When he switched the phone back on, he got the message about the funeral. He rang the library, but they couldn't find me, and he couldn't drive to the university to find me. By the time I

Chapter 3 – Displaced
Changing Roles

arrived home, late that afternoon, the funeral was over. I would have gone for my Dad's sake, even though he was deceased at the time. Looking back now, maybe I was saved from something I didn't need to do.

Now that he didn't have the constraints of a full-time job, Kola had another dream. He wanted to travel around Australia. We bought a large caravan and began to prepare. I was still teaching full-time. We put our lovely home up for sale. It wasn't long before we had a buyer. The whole process, however, had been quite unpleasant, from the pushy, bossy real-estate agent to the solicitors of the purchaser. The legal firm issued us with an account for legal fees.

We did our own legal work so did not need nor solicit help. They were adamant we pay them. We were adamant we would not, and we did not.

We had put the house on the market for $10,000 more than we had paid for it. The man who was to buy had an accident and withdrew from the sale. Six months later we sold the property for $40,000 more than what we had paid for it. God is good, but sometimes we are so blinded by circumstances, we just don't see it.

On the Road

It was my birthday when we closed the door of our home for the last time and drove away. Our furniture was in storage and the caravan packed and ready to go. I loved our home and garden, but that season in our lives was finished. Sadness at leaving my home, teaching and friends was tempered by anticipation of what lay ahead. We were all excited at the beginning of our journey.

We did not have a four-wheel-drive, but our Ford Fairmont car was roomy and comfortable. Kola had a switch attached so that we could use either petrol or gas. He also had a device fitted which enabled us to refill the gas bottles for the fridge and stove. We had back-up batteries for our lights and other equipment.

Our caravan was eighteen-feet long by eight-feet wide. Our bedroom was at the front. A window stretched all the way along the front of the van. Kola and I both had our own bedside table and drawers, and we had a shared wardrobe. There was storage space under the bed where I kept our winter clothes and doonas, blankets etc. As you walked into the caravan, our bedroom was to the left. To the right was our kitchen/dining room/school room. We had a good-sized fridge, full-sized oven and cook top and ample storage for food and utensils. The table ran lengthwise along the wall next to the door. A large window was behind the table, giving us lots of light when the boys were doing their schoolwork.

The schoolwork was stored under the seats in individual containers. At the end of the van were triple bunks, each with cupboards at the head of their beds and a wardrobe to store clothes, skateboards, racquets and whatever else our boys needed. A folding vinyl door separated the boys' room from the rest of the van.

Because we all slept in a confined space, we could hear the boys in their beds at the opposite end of the van. One night, Luke fell out of his bed on the top bunk. It was quite a long way to fall. We rushed to him, and Kola lifted him and put him back to bed. He didn't wake up, and in the morning, had no recollection of having fallen, no bruises, no sore spots. He was so deeply asleep and relaxed when he fell that for him it was as though it never happened. For us it meant some quick reconstruction to make sure it wasn't repeated.

Another night Luke talked in his sleep. 'The cats are in the cupboard.'

'What are they doing?' I asked.

'What cats like to do, best.'

'What do cats like to do best?'

He rolled over and that was the end of the conversation. We asked him again in the morning, but of course he had no memory of the conversation, so we never did find out what the cats were doing. Come to that, we didn't have any cats, but we did have our dog, Laddie, a beautiful three-year old tricolour collie rough like Lassie. He travelled at my feet in the car by day and slept on the floor at the end of our bed by night.

I was very organised. Everything had a place, and everything was kept in place when not in use. My washing machine was an upright plastic container with a lid which sealed tight. I would load it up, add washing powder and screw on the lid. As we travelled the motion of the car and van agitated the water. When we pulled up to camp, I would wash everything by hand and hang it out often draping it out over trees and bushes, I washed every day, so never had the washing back up on me.

As we bush-camped for almost all of the three-and-a-half-years we travelled, the water was often bucketed out of a creek where we camped. We did not have a shower in the caravan, but we had two camp showers. These were plastic bags, clear on one side, black plastic on the other. On sunny days, we lay them on the ground or on the car bonnet, filled with water, which would then heat up from the sun. Sometimes the water got

Chapter 3 – Displaced
On the Road

so hot, that we would put out only one of the bags to heat, and add the hot water to cold in the second bag till we had the temperature we wanted. Kola would then suspend the bag by a hook to the top of the van and the bottom of the bag had a shower nozzle attached so that we all had warm showers. We had a screen fixed to give us privacy.

At one campsite in Western Australia, out in the middle of nowhere, there were about ten of us. The heat during the day was unbearable. A big dish was placed on the ground and all of us recycled the shower water in an attempt to get cool.

It was most unhygienic, but we did what we had to do. None of us got sick, by some miracle and we all survived the extreme heat of that day.

We packed a library of books for the boys to read which included Enid Blyton's *Faraway Tree* series, C. S. Lewis' *Narnia* series, Laura Ingalls-Wilder's *Little House on the Prairie* series, Tolkien's *Lord of the Rings* trilogy and other series of books. We read them all over the course of our trip. Kola would read to the boys or we would take turns to read. When we stayed in a town for a week or more, we would access the local library.

Kola began a game, which the boys loved. They were all given different names. Tim became Mitta, Jonathon became Noj and Luke became Aluk. Kola would begin the story, then each of us would take turns to tell the next bit. They had such adventures travelling into space, to the centre of the earth, to the depths of the ocean or into wild jungles, fighting enemies and always coming out victorious.

Although we had the stove in the caravan, we often cooked over a campfire, wrapping damper dough around sticks and cooking them over hot coals, then coating them in margarine and golden syrup or honey. On other occasions, we cooked damper loaves or hot, wholesome stews in the camp oven. We would wrap potatoes and corn in foil and let them cook in the coals of the campfire. A favourite recipe was date rolls, the mixture spooned into empty baked-bean tins and allowed to cook in the camp oven, which was partly filled with water. The lid would be put on and the rolls would steam over the hot coals till cooked.

Kola's favourite meal to cook was homemade pizza. He'd make the dough, roll it out, cook it, and then load it up with all sorts of yummy toppings.

As we travelled, we got to know others who were on the same route. Campsite to campsite we would meet up again and then have wonderful combined meals sitting around a campfire, with the stars above us, as we'd share our adventures. Most days fitted into a routine - breakfast, make beds, tidy up, schoolwork, then we'd be ready to explore.

During our three-and-a half years on the road, we had some wonderful experiences.

Our first night on the road we pulled into a campsite in the mountains. It was August and freezing. We hadn't thought of a heater, so I closed the van up, drew the curtains, turned the oven on and opened the oven door. I pulled out a couple of candles and lit them instead of using the van lights. It was awesome. The van warmed quickly, and the candlelight made us feel like we were pioneers setting out on our adventure.

One of the first places we explored was the Burning Mountain at Wingen, New South Wales. An underground coal seam has been burning for thousands of years. As we left the car park, a couple of plovers dive-bombed us. The female hatches her chicks in a depression in the grass. The male keeps watch and attacks anyone who poses a threat.

They have spurs on the tips of their wings and if they get you it can really hurt. Armed with a stick each, we got out of the car park and progressed up the mountain.

Sheep were grazing in the paddock. Laddie immediately went into sheepdog mode and began to round up a sheep. (He used to herd our chooks at home!). The sheep took off up the track with Laddie at her heels and us in close pursuit behind. The poor sheep fell and was lying on its

Chapter 3 – Displaced
On the Road

back. Laddie looked at the sheep as if to say 'that's not part of the game'. We hoisted the sheep onto her feet again, put Laddie on his lead and continued up the mountain.

Hot sulphurous fumes rose up from the earths' depths where large cracks had opened. Boardwalks had been erected so that visitors could walk safely over the scorched earth. Along the ridge of the mountain we found seashells. It was amazing! Seashells on a mountain ridge, way inland!

Arriving in Glen Innes, New South Wales we found a flyer for a day trip on an old restored steam train to Guyra and back. Kola parked our car and van on the street across from the railway station because we couldn't fit in the station car park. The boys were bouncing around everywhere, unable to contain their excitement. This was a totally new experience for them. The rattling and swaying of the train, the drifting smoke from the train's furnace and the open windows from which they could view the passing countryside, plus lunch and morning and afternoon tea made the day really special.

It was late when we arrived back, and the boys were weary and ready for bed. We decided we would sleep in the van where it was and move on the next day. The next morning, we all woke early, had breakfast, made the beds and cleaned up. The boys were all sitting around the table doing schoolwork, while I completed my tasks, when there was a knock on the door. Opening it, I found a policeman at the door. We invited him in. He was very apologetic for disturbing us. The old lady in the house, in front of which we'd parked, had complained to the police about us being there. Apparently, she was always ringing them up complaining about something or other. Our policeman sat and talked to us all for a while and then gave us an invitation. 'Why don't you come down to the station? We've a museum there in the old station house.'

The boys loved it. They took turns in the lock-up and were fingerprinted. The police all added to our total experience of Glen Innes. That old lady did us all a huge favour by complaining.

Though the Storms Rage
Yet Will I Dance

And so, we progressed around Australia.

At Inskip Point, just south of Frazer Island, Queensland, we sat through a cyclone. We could not start our car to get out. Our caravan was parked end-on against a high dune, which saved us from harm. The wind hit the dune and lifted up and over our van. Had we been a little further away from the dune, or side-on to it, the wind would have lifted us. We sat in the van and prayed for safety. We were kept safe. The van shook, the wind roared but we were safe. We sat looking out of our big window. The wind stopped abruptly as though a tap had been turned off. The storm was gone. The next morning, we wandered along the beach. Debris from the storm lay everywhere.

That day we picked up beautiful shells which had been tossed onto the beach. We also found a small seahorse, a sea dragon and several different kinds of starfish. We also found a toothbrush, comb, a plate and other objects and we wondered if some small craft and its occupants had come to grief during the night.

Victoria River in the north of Western Australia was magical. We pulled up parallel to the river and sat in our van, looking out of our big window. It was not safe to go out once it was dark, as saltwater crocodiles inhabited the water and the banks. The river was also home to sharks, stingrays, and various fish. There is phosphorescence in the water. Although it was dark, we could see the movement of all these creatures, as they dived, circled and moved through the water.

For six weeks, we camped in a tiny fishing village in South Australia. Parry's Beach was home to a group of tuna fisherman and their families. Power was provided by generator. A lookout was perched high on the second set of dunes. A couple of the fishermen would keep watch there waiting for a shadow to move across the water. Such a shadow signalled a school of tuna passing by. The watchman would then pick up the phone, which set off an alarm back in the village, waking the crew. Racing down to the beach, a boat would set out, dragging a net from a

Chapter 3 – Displaced
On the Road

tractor. The boat would circle the fish and then return to shore to a second tractor.

Both tractors would then pull the laden net into shore where everyone, fishermen and tourists alike, would throw the fish onto a conveyor belt, which then deposited the catch into waiting trucks. Those of us who helped would be given a fish to take back to camp to cook or smoke. This meant that we had fresh fish every day for six weeks. Luke spent many mornings up in the watchtower doing his schoolwork with the help of Sam, a wonderful old, wizened fisherman.

Our experiences were wide and varied: From exploring the sand dunes, caves, holes, cliffs and abandoned homesteads on the Nullarbor, to the crystal water, coloured corals and tropical fish of the Great Barrier Reef, far north Queensland. From watching an approaching bushfire lighting up the sky at the end of the road at Kalbarri, Western Australia, knowing that if it wasn't halted, our only escape was the ocean; and then seeing wild flowers burst into bloom from the midst of the blackened earth. From the hot, blue-green water and lush growth of Mataranka Springs in the Northern Territory to the cold mountain creeks and fold upon fold of mountains in the Snowy Mountains of New South Wales.

During our three-year journey, we saw and experienced much. Tim's dream to visit Turkey was birthed at Mataranka when we camped with four young British tourists who shared their experiences with us. Both Tim and Jonathon have now fulfilled this dream. The boys and I have all travelled overseas now, visiting many countries and cultures.

For me, however, there was a growing unrest and unhappiness. Kola and I were both struggling but not communicating in a good way. Kola wanted me to go on the dole. I did not. My Dad had taught me, 'If you don't work, you don't eat'. I was fiercely independent. I sank lower and lower into depression until the only good times for me were when I was teaching in a school somewhere. I taught in many schools around Australia.

Though the Storms Rage
Yet Will I Dance

At Tamworth High, the students wanted to hear about our adventures and worked very hard for me, finishing units of work early, so that I could take them outside and tell them of our exploits. Once I was called to the office to pick up my camera which Kola had just bought and delivered to the school. Another teacher stayed in the classroom and was amazed when students dictated my notes and continued to write, completing the work by the time I returned to the classroom.

While at West Wyalong High, south west New South Wales, I had been given a dance class to teach. Knowing nothing about dance, I feared I was heading for disaster. As I gathered my class in the hall, a young girl who I had taught in English classes was standing sullenly by the stage. I was in a state of mild panic. 'Do you know this dance?'

'Yes.'

'Why aren't you with your class?'

'I'm in trouble. I have to stay here.'

'Will you teach this dance to my class please?

'Yes.'

She took over, getting the students positioned and put on the tape. She was a born teacher, and the class was a resounding success. If anyone put a foot out of place, she was onto him or her. The class responded, and all I had to do was stand by and watch this young girl teach. She was known as a troublesome student, but for me she really tried in her English class.

I went to the principal and told him what had happened. This young girl got a special award at the next assembly. I hope this experience was the impetus she needed to set a goal and get her life back on track. I was offered a permanent position at the school, and when I left after six weeks, was given a farewell as though I had been there for years.

....

Chapter 3 – Displaced
On the Road

Although my teaching was going well, conversation between Kola and I had all but ceased. There were no more loving, caring words or actions, only criticism and condemnation. During school hours, I taught. Back at the van I handwashed endless loads of dirty clothes. I became increasingly more isolated and I cried a lot. There were days when I could not stop crying. We were on the road. There was no-one I could turn to for help. I yearned for my home, to get my hands dirty in my garden, to see my pictures on the wall, and to sit and lose myself at my piano. I didn't have my garden, so filled my van with wildflowers picked along the road. I didn't have my pictures on the wall, but I took endless photos. I didn't have my piano, but I had my guitar and taught myself to play classical guitar.

I loved teaching and these teaching episodes provided me with an escape which enabled me to keep going, despite my unhappiness. One school which offered me ways out of my predicament was Tennant Creek High School.

Tennant Creek is a small mining town in the centre of Australia, north of Alice Springs. We arrived in the town in July during mid-winter. The nights were cool, but the days were warm. I approached the high school to see if they had any relief teaching available. They were desperate for a teacher because two of their teachers were absent long-term. One teacher had hit a buffalo on his way home from Alice Springs and was badly injured. Another teacher was due to have her baby.

At the end of the term was the annual concert, so I was employed immediately, and the school re-arranged the timetable giving me music classes to help prepare for the upcoming concert. As the weeks progressed, we set up extra rehearsal times preparing for the concert. I was happy as the concert date drew near and we had a good program of well-rehearsed items to present.

One day during a spare period I went into the school library and found some pictures books containing photos of Uluru (a large monolith in Central Australia) and other scenes around the area.

Though the Storms Rage
Yet Will I Dance

I sat on a beanbag with the books scattered around me, looking for good angles and special places that I could access when taking my own photos. A group of aboriginal children came into the library with another young teacher. When they saw me, they abandoned him and instead gathered themselves around me on the floor. Turning the page, there was a photo of an aboriginal man swinging a snake in the air. Excitedly one of the boys pointed to the photo and in a mix of his dialect and English told me his Dad did this to break the back of the snake and kill it, and then they would cook it over the fire.

'Miss, you must come. We cook a feast for you!'

I motioned for their teacher to join us. Although none of these students had been to a city or were ever likely to do so, this straight-out-of-college teacher had set them an assignment on a city to do. I knew too, that this young man had several resignation letters which as yet he had not submitted, pinned to the cork board behind his desk in the staff room. Pointing to the photo, which excited our young students, I looked at the teacher.

'This is what you should set for them. Get them to do a project on their own culture!'

Not long after this, I walked to the shops in the main street, during a free period. An old bare-footed aboriginal woman approached me and called me 'Daughter'. I have never felt so honoured as I did that day.

At Tennant Creek High school, I co-taught an aboriginal class with another teacher. He was a kind, gentle man, about my age, who I will call Jim. I taught side by side with him during the six weeks I was there and we became good friends. Our class was an aboriginal class. The students came into school from a reserve just out of town. Frequently, different students would be absent, so we taught basic English to these young people. They were beautiful people to be with. We had two adjoining rooms which we could open up into one area and Jim and I moved amongst them, as we taught. A lot of individual assistance was needed, hence the need to work

Chapter 3 – Displaced
On the Road

as a team. We worked together almost every day. I can't remember specifically talking to Jim of my unhappiness. I guess I must have let something slip. It would be hard not to, working in such close proximity for that period of time.

While I was primarily involved in the music of the school, Jim was involved in drama. Both were integral to the annual school concert. He was a single man. I was married, but desperately unhappy in my marriage. I craved for acceptance, kindness and gentleness. I was longing for male companionship. I was not getting this from my husband, but in our easy relationship which developed within the confines of the school, this caring man met those needs. I was drawn to him. Jim belonged to a local drama group and invited me to join him at the drama meetings after school. Although I would dearly have liked to accept his invitation, I never did. We were two lonely people working together and our friendship had the potential to become a deep one. Our feelings were mutual.

Towards the end of the six weeks, he asked me to stay with him in Tennant Creek and at the end of the year to go back to Adelaide with him. It was a huge invitation. It was a way out of my unhappiness. Two things prevented me from accepting his invitation. Firstly, despite my misery, I believed in the sanctity of my marriage vows. Secondly, and equally important, I would never separate my three boys from their father.

The concert was a great success. The aboriginal children, all wanted to be in a photo with me. Jim had offered me an escape, as did the school, for they offered me a permanent position at the school.

At the end of my last day at school, Jim walked with me to the gate. I knew this would be the last time I would see him, but I had made my decision. I was torn as I got into the car next to Kola. My boys were sitting in the back seat. I turned towards Jim and we waved goodbye. Sometimes I wonder what my life would have been like if I had accepted either of these offers, but I also know that I made the right decision.

Descent into Despair

During our time on the road, we'd removed ourselves from our family, friends and trusted social networks. We'd also grown distant from God because of the hurt from our last church. With no one to turn to, I came to a place of total despair. We were camped in a free campsite out of town with no facilities except toilets and a tap. I had approached the local schools of the city we were near and between two schools I had a month's work booked up. Coming home from school I approached Kola while he was talking to another man, who was also camped where we were.

'There is a caravan park nearby. I want us to go there so that I can use the washing machines.'

'No, we are fine here.'

I argued back. 'I am the one financing this trip by teaching. I am sick of having to teach and then come home and handwash for five people every day. We are going into the caravan park!'

The man standing by began mocking me, so I turned on him. 'Mind your own business and get back to your own wife and van.' He left, and that night we moved into the caravan park, but instead of things improving, they deteriorated even more. Kola became very angry and morose because he believed he had lost his freedom and it was my fault.

I had had enough. I got a packet of twenty-four painkillers and swallowed the lot. I had reached a point of total desolation and desperation and I wanted to end my life.

I know that writing about this episode in my life, there will be some who will condemn me. I can only say to those critics, 'You can't judge people unless you have walked totally in their shoes'.

Though the Storms Rage
Yet Will I Dance

For those who have attempted suicide or are contemplating it, I will say to you, 'I understand where you are, and I know your total despair. I understand because I have been there. I too have walked that road.

All I needed was someone to be there for me, to wrap their arms around me, to listen without judgment, to offer hope, to be a friend.

Having taken the overdose of painkillers, I looked at my boys and realised I didn't want to die. I had my boys. 'Oh God, what have I done? 'I told Kola what had happened and asked him to take me to hospital.

Jonathon, my second son, has written about this from his eyes and I will share it with you now.

"My father, who always loved travelling, decided that we would sell our home and travel Australia in our Ford Fairmont and our caravan. So, for three and a half years we travelled – Mum, Dad us three brothers, and our beautiful Collie dog Laddie. (Thankfully, we had sold at the height of a property boom, and then banked the money when interest was earning up to 18%). This brought many highs and lows.

We were home-schooled, and many times we would pull up next to some magnificent location, like tropical Palm Cove next to Cairns in Queensland and spend a couple weeks exploring and swimming through coral caves, while studying in our caravan overlooking a tropical paradise with white sand and perfect weather. Or exploring caves along the Nullarbor Plain where we three brothers almost got lost in the sand-dune deserts, coming home just on dark to our panicking parents. But the lows were very low indeed. On top of not having any friends except one another (since we were constantly moving from place to place for almost 4 years), my parents fought a lot. At one point, my mum had had enough of the travelling and life itself and decided to end her life by overdosing on painkillers, while my broken father just looked on. My brothers and I were witnessing everything from the back of our small caravan and were crying and pleading with them to do something – anything, to make things right. But what does an 11-year-

Chapter 3 – Displaced
Descent into Despair

old know? We just didn't want our mum to die! Eventually, after maybe an hour or so, dad took mum to the hospital in the nearest city where the doctors gave her medicine to help her expel the Panadol, leaving my brothers and I in the caravan by ourselves that night. This was one of our darkest nights, one of many.

Eventually, after travelling the length and breadth of this big country, my mum finally convinced dad that we kids needed to settle down and get an education in preparation for life beyond the road. So, we took the long drive back from Perth to Brisbane, where we entered public schools, Tim into grade 11, me into grade 9, and Luke into grade 6, while still living in a caravan on a property outside of Caboolture."

It would be great to say I came home from hospital, Kola and I sorted out our problems and life became wonderful. In reality, that is very far from the truth. We were a long way from God and from each other, and we had no one to turn to due to our itinerant lifestyle.

I was asked recently by a friend, 'How did you dance through this period?' I didn't dance. This is the one time in my life when I almost gave up. Instead of dancing, I limped. I loved my sons and knew that I needed to keep going for them. I taught, looked after my family and did all the necessary things. Communication with Kola was still closed. We did not understand each other. I believe we still loved each other, but neither of us knew how to deal with what life had handed us.

I am, in essence, a very strong person and I built a resolve to be there for my boys regardless of everything. I still cried a lot. I was still in despair, but I knew that I had to do something to survive. I didn't have anyone to share with, so I poured out my heart, my fears, my feelings and my deepest needs into my journal. I have always written and will keep on doing so.

I continued playing my guitar, arranging wildflowers and collecting shells. One day I saw some long-stitch packs in a craft shop and

Though the Storms Rage
Yet Will I Dance

bought one. It was of a beautiful old cottage surrounded by a garden. That was the first of several, which I did.

If indeed I did dance through that period, it was a very hesitant broken dance. I can't help thinking of the dance of the dying swan in Tchaikowsky's *Swan Lake* ballet. Even in the midst of deepest grief there is a poignancy and beauty. Unlike that beautiful swan, I did not die (although I came close to doing so) but rose from that despair. My journey upwards from despair still had a long way to go, but at least I was heading in the right direction again.

Chapter 3 Displaced ~ For Reflection

1. Have you ever felt displaced or that you didn't belong? Have you ever felt cut off from family and friends? Can you share how you felt and why, to someone you trust?

2. The world is full of displaced people—refugees, people made redundant from their jobs, children removed from their families and homes. The list goes on! Do you know someone who may be in this situation? What can you do to help?

3. Because of family circumstances, redundancy, illness or some other reason, have you had to change roles within your family? Would you like to share what this feels like and what your friends could do to ease your journey?

4. Have you ever contemplated suicide? Is there someone you can speak to, even if it's a helpline? Speaking to someone can help remove the isolation and despair you are feeling.

5. Do you know anyone in any of the above situations? Can you be that someone who can wrap your arms around him/her, listen without judgement, offer hope and be a friend?

Chapter 4 – Into the Valley Again

1. Diagnosis
2. Remission
3. Cancer Returns
4. Returning to God
5. Forgiveness
6. Love Letters
7. Saying Goodbye

Diagnosis

Kola stood in the kitchen, shirtless, slowly tracing his fingers across his stomach. A mass of what appeared to be swollen glands distended his abdomen. More glands were swollen under his armpits.

A trip to the doctor raised more alarm bells. 'I will book you in immediately. You must go and have a scan and ultrasound.'

'But it is probably just a virus which will go away,' Kola said.

'No. You must go and have the scan and you must go NOW!'

We looked at each other, silent, as fear was birthed in the pit of our stomachs. For years now, we had barely spoken to each other; married, but living separate lives.

After travelling around Australia for three years, we settled in Caboolture, Queensland, where our three boys went to school. I continued to do relief teaching while establishing a private music school. Not long after settling in Caboolture, Kola came out in a rash and developed a fever. Soon the disabling pain and exhaustion of Ross River virus became the daily norm for Kola. Tim, Jonathon and I contracted glandular fever. Luke was the only one of our family who did not get sick. I kept teaching because someone had to earn an income. I was exhausted and my legs ached, but I needed to press on. Bills had to be paid and food put on the table.

The Ross River virus morphed into Chronic Fatigue. Kola struggled to keep going.

Tim and I got better while Jonathon became worse. Eventually Jonathon was diagnosed with Gilbert's Syndrome – a hepatitis-like illness, which turned his skin and the whites of his eyes yellow. His body was producing too much bilirubin and his liver struggled to function properly. He had to leave school and continue learning at home, through distance education. Now, Kola and I found ourselves in a diagnostic centre where Kola underwent tests.

'You have Non-Hodgkin's Lymphoma – Stage 4.' Tears welled in our eyes. We went home. The boys were still at school. Now, after years of not talking to each other, the threat and reality of cancer did what nothing else had been able to do. We talked. We acknowledged our fears, we acknowledged our years of struggle and we acknowledged our love for each other and for our three precious sons.

Kola had not long turned fifty. His mother, Ludmilla, had died of cancer only fifteen years earlier, also aged fifty. That memory hammered home the reality of where this cancer could take us. We remembered, too, how lonely her death had been. Kola's Dad forbade anyone to tell her she was dying.

I remember staying with her at home while her husband and sons went to the doctors to get results about her condition. She had lost the ability to speak, but held her hands together as though in prayer and pointed to me and back to herself.

I hugged her and prayed, and it drew us into a deep bond for which I will forever be grateful. When the three men returned, they acknowledged us but gave no information. She looked pleadingly at me, causing me to react.

'Surely there is something you can tell her. She has waited all day. For goodness sake, say something. You can't do this to her.'

I can't remember what was said, but I know she was not told the truth about her illness. She had been given only eight weeks to live but nobody told her.

Ludmilla was an attractive, warm, intuitive and intelligent woman. When she hit this brick wall of silence, she worked it out for herself, but the utter tragedy of it was that she could not communicate with anyone. She reacted by shutting herself off from her husband, so now we had two

Chapter 4 – Into the Valley Again
Diagnosis

people living in lonely isolation at a time in their lives when they so desperately needed each other. There was no communication, no words, no hugs, nothing.

Learning from that tragic mistake, we went home, gathered our three sons, and we told them the truth. Communication lines were opened and we all helped each other through this valley into which we had just entered.

Kola's treatment progressed with him taking chemotherapy, in tablet form and cortisone tablets. He was monitored by regular blood tests. I bought him a sheep fleece under-blanket and new pyjamas. We put a CD/radio player in the bedroom and made the room a happy welcoming place. We talked and laughed and sometimes cried.

At one stage bindi-weed sprouted everywhere in the lawn, and Kola got out there with a hand-held two-pronged weeding tool and diligently plucked out the weed by the bucketful. He associated each bindi-weed as a cancer cell. It was laborious work, but it was also a positive action. He would beat this.

Remission

After two and a half years Kola was in remission. We rejoiced in this reprieve.

One day Kola took himself off to a car auction and came home with a beautifully restored Triumph Stag convertible sports car. He was like a little boy with his Christmas stocking. He didn't go with the intention of buying a car, but it was there, and he bought it. All three boys now had a driver's licence. Luke, our youngest, was seventeen. That car, nearly always with the roof rolled back allowing the wind to ruffle our hair, provided hours and hours of fun and excitement for all of our family.

Kola and I would often make the half-hour drive to Bribie Island at sunrise and walk along the wave-washed sand as the sun rose over the water.

Possums arriving back to their holes in the gum trees along the esplanade would argue with the cockatoos and galahs for residency of a particular home. They all nested in hollow branches high in the trees. We would often see dolphins at play in the sparkling water just off shore. When the water was warm enough, Kola would swim, while I paddled along the edge of the waves. While walking along the beach, early one morning, Kola looked out to the ocean, then turned to me.

'This is where I want my ashes scattered, in the ocean, free. Please, if I die, will you scatter my ashes here?'

It was a hard thing to listen to. He was alive. He hated being boxed in. He loved the ocean, and he loved the quietness and remoteness of this stretch of beach. Quietly, I gave him my promise. 'Yes, I will. The boys and I together will do this for you.'

In September 1998, Kola and I went on a mini-holiday. It was like a second honeymoon. Indeed, it was the only time in twenty-four years of

Though the Storms Rage
Yet Will I Dance

marriage that we had a holiday without our boys. We packed up our camping gear and headed to Hervey Bay, about three hours north of where we lived. We wandered through the main street of Maryborough with its elegant old buildings, before crossing the coastal plain to Hervey Bay where we boarded a whale-watching ship. The boat was two storeys high, so we made our way to the top deck. We cruised along the shoreline of Frazer Island (a large sand island off the Queensland Coast) and waited for the whales (mothers and their babies) to make an appearance.

We didn't have to wait long before those gentle giants of the ocean began to breach out of the water and come along close to our ship. I am sure they were just as curious of us, as we were of them. At the end of the day we found a campsite and bedded down for the night.

We broke camp the next morning and headed home. Packed carefully into our case was a photo of the two of us taken while on board the ship.

Cancer Returns

A week after our holiday away, pain in Kolas' back made us return to the doctor. Tests soon revealed that the lymphoma had returned. Now it was not just in the lymph system but had spread to his bones. The cancer this time was far more aggressive than the first time and required radical treatment.

A few months earlier, Kola had seen short courses in writing advertised at the University of Queensland and had booked me in to do four of these courses. In one subject, the instructor, a published author, told us to use our dreams as springboards or ideas for our writing. I replied at the time that I didn't dream, or if I did, I certainly had no memory of them. A few days after this class, I was awoken by a very vivid dream which became the subject of my next assignment. It was written at the beginning of this period of our life and gives one aspect of how we were able to 'dance in the rain' during this particular storm. I would like to share with you now.

A Fortune Cookie and A Dream

Trees closed in threateningly, reaching out as though to ensnare me. It was overcast, and dark, not really daylight, more a half-light. I screamed and fought in fear and panic as I was being dragged relentlessly and mercilessly along a corrugated and stony dirt road. The sharp stones tore at my flesh and the red dust coated my wounds. My clothes were shredded and my tears joined with the dirt and the blood, coating my body in its own war-paint.

I didn't recognise the road. I didn't see who or what was dragging me. I was being dragged I knew not where by a force I did not know.

In the still of the night, I awoke, troubled and disturbed, and I lay in my bed thinking of this dream, which broke my sleep.

Though the Storms Rage
Yet Will I Dance

It wasn't difficult to relate my dream to the reality of my life. My husband's two and a half years of remission had come to an end. The cancer was back and once again we were thrown into the treadmill of scans, biopsies, pain, morphine drips and chemotherapy.

As we progressed through the two weeks of diagnostic tests, our lives were devastated. All control was seemingly lost and we sank into deep despair. Pain, fear, tears, sleeplessness, became our lot.

During this time, I thought of a story I was supposed to write. It was based on a quote found in a Chinese fortune cookie, and read like this:-

'People find it difficult to resist your persuasive manner.'

I had received this quote, just one week before these two weeks of tests began. At the time I thought,

'I can't write about this. I don't regard myself as a particularly persuasive individual.'

However, as the following weeks progressed, I had a lot of time to think. Nights when I should have been asleep, I thought. The hours spent sitting beside Kola in hospital, or waiting in sterile rooms while Kola underwent test after test, I had time to think.

My fortune cookie quote and my dream became linked. I now knew what was dragging me.

I knew what road I was on, and I knew how persuasive the voice of cancer could be. I determined that it was not going to have total control, and with this I set about controlling everything that I had the power to control. I rostered my family into meal preparation, washing up, lawn mowing. I rearranged my teaching schedule, worked with Kola, my husband, through the many appointments and tests and the hospitalisation. Because my time and energy were in short supply, I let everybody know what was happening and requested that my friends not contact me, rather let me do the contacting when needed.

Chapter 4 – Into the Valley Again
Cancer Returns

Now Kola is undergoing multiple treatments of chemotherapy, and his pain is being controlled. He is positive about the outcome.

Yesterday, we went for an early morning walk along the beach. The waves glowed pink in the sunrise and parrots chattered noisily in the trees, and we felt at peace.

Yes, the cancer is still dragging us down a road we don't want to walk, and yes the cancer still has a persuasive voice, but it does not have total control. We are resisting, and while we still must walk the road, we now know that we have a choice as to how we will walk it.

Returning to God

We had turned our backs on God in 1986 when we left the church to which we had belonged and served.

Even after Kola was diagnosed with cancer and the ensuing three and a half years, even though we went through hard times, we independently soldiered on, still not seeking God.

The cancer returned in the same month. It was also that month that I had my first dream which I recorded in 'A Fortune Cookie and a Dream'. The dreams kept coming and I found myself waking between 2.00 am and 3.00 am every morning. I had an intense need to call out to God and ask Him to empty me of myself. I did not understand it, but I could not ignore it. Several times during the day I repeated the prayer, 'God, empty me of myself'. This imperative to pray this prayer continued for six months. The waking between 2.00 am and 3.00 am became routine and I found myself looking forward to this precious hour when it was just God and me.

Often, an image of a person's face would be shown me and I knew I was to pray for that person. I didn't know them, nor in most cases, the need of that person. I would just take them to God.

'God, you know that person and you know her need. I give her to you and ask you to meet her where she is and help her.'

I didn't know it then, but Kola was on a similar journey. One Friday night in early March 1999, Kola and I held hands and prayed. It was thirteen years since we had prayed together. It is never the wrong time, nor too late to call out to God.

Not long before that, I'd started reading my bible again. I reread the story of the prodigal son. He had taken his inheritance and had left his father's home. He wasted his money on worthless pursuits until the day came that he had nothing left. He decided to return home. Maybe he could get a job as a servant on his father's farm. The most wonderful part of the story is this. While he was still a long way off, his father, who was standing at the gate and looking down the road, recognised his son and ran to embrace him.

The waking up at 2.00 am each morning, the prayer placed in my heart to empty myself of me, and the dreams which showed me the path we were on and how to walk it -all came from my heavenly Father. While we walked away, he stood at the gate, gently calling us home. Thirteen years was not too long for God to wait, nor is twenty or fifty or seventy or more years. Father God is standing at the gate, waiting, and He is ever so gently calling, 'Come home, Come home'.

We had been very badly hurt by church people. Now we had come home to God, we needed a Christian church or group where we could worship and fellowship. More importantly, we needed to find someone we could trust and who could mentor us.

We went onto the internet looking for a particular person and in the process found an article written by another man, a former lecturer of Kola's.

This dear man, Eion, his wife and family had also been displaced and badly hurt by the same organisation which had hurt us. He was on a very different path, but a path ordained by his God.

He had gone to a healing service with his daughter, where his granddaughter, then only a baby, was healed of a severe neurological condition that had resulted in convulsions and rigidity of her little body. A woman sitting in front of them asked to hold the baby. She took the child and raised her arms with the baby in her hands. As she lifted the child, the baby's rigid body relaxed and became like those of a normal baby. She was completely healed and remains so to this day. She is now a normal, active young adult completing her tertiary education.

Meanwhile our friend felt as though his stomach was on fire. The speaker said that there was a man in the audience with a fire in his belly.

Chapter 4 – Into the Valley Again
Returning to God

That man was to get up and go to the stage. This he did. Our friend was told that he was going to be sacked from the ministry he was in, but that God was calling him into a healing ministry.

Not long after returning home, the elder of his church was diagnosed with cancer. No treatment was helping to cure it. Turning to his wife, our friend said, 'We must go and lay hands on him and claim healing'. They did that and the elder was immediately and completely healed. Our friend was forthwith sacked from the ministry which had been his life. He walked into a healing ministry which took him to Africa, India, the United States and Australia. He witnessed many healings, including cancers dropping off of bodies, limbs growing, deaf ears opening and blind eyes seeing.

I wrote to him and he promptly contacted us.

For six months, either he or his wife rang us from America nearly every day, praying with us and mentoring us. A short time later, he came to Australia. Gathering a small team of four, they spent fourteen hours travelling from Sydney, New South Wales to our home in Caboolture, Queensland. We bedded them down on makeshift mattresses on the floor, for at the time we had no spare beds. We had told some close friends of the healing meeting we were to have in our home. When the time came we had about twelve people in our lounge room.

Outside, we were experiencing the heaviest rain for years and our yard was totally awash. The torrential rain on the roof was deafening but inside an even heavier rain began to fall on us. As our friend spoke and prayed with us, the rain of the Holy Spirit fell, and we were changed.

Tim and his friend were just curious, but as they were touched by the Holy Spirit, their hearts were changed. They were both freed of their drug addiction to marijuana, without even a hint of withdrawal symptoms, and they gave their lives to God.

Though the Storms Rage
Yet Will I Dance

Jonathon, in the solitude of his bedroom, had said to God, 'If you want me to believe in you, you need to do something that logic cannot explain!'

That night we had what is called a 'gold anointing'. Up until that point we had never heard of such a thing. Our friends had brought with them a video from a church in Toronto, Canada where the gold anointing had been happening. As we watched it, people's fillings in their teeth were being changed into gold fillings.

We were told, 'If you want this, place your hand on your mouth.' Jonathon received a gold filling, and I watched as Kola's teeth fillings changed from amalgam to gold. I did not want gold in my mouth, but I had it in my hair, my face and eyebrows and my hands. It was a source of wonder.

What effect did it have on us?

Jonathon fell into the arms of God, all skepticism and doubt gone. He has been in full-time effective ministry now for many years.

Kola would ask me to hold a small hand-mirror for him so that he could see the gold fillings. It was an encouragement to him, that God loved him.

For me, it was a special gift of the favour of God. As the night progressed, I was filled with His Holy Spirit. It was like an electric current passing through me. My body tingled, and the following morning I held my hands up in wonder. They were still tingling. God had me praying for six months to be emptied of myself. Now He had filled me with His Spirit. I was now in peace and had courage to face the future. We, like the prodigal son, had returned home.

Forgiveness

Although we had come back to God, there was one big issue in Kola's life to be dealt with.

Unforgiveness and its resultant bitterness still lay heavy on his heart. He was unable to forgive the church for how it had wronged and hurt him.

Three years previously, Pastor Murray from the local church came to our house. Kola recognised him, but shut the door in his face. The pastor could do nothing else but walk away. A couple of weeks later, I received a phone call from Murray.

'Marion, would you teach our daughter to play the piano?'

'Yes, of course I will. I would like to teach your daughter.'

Murray would bring his daughter each week for her lesson, but he would stay in his car until we were finished. Then I would go out and speak to him. We had been students together when I did my education/music degree and he completed his theology degree. His parents and mine had been good friends. I had nothing against him. I liked Murray, his family and his parents very much. His daughter was a good student. Kola knew I was teaching Murray's daughter, and that I talked to him, but for Kola it was a closed book.

While Murray had done him no wrong, Kola saw him as a representative of the organisation which had wronged him. He was not ready to forgive.

Skip forward to May 1999 when Kola was admitted into the Royal Brisbane Hospital. The radical treatment which we hoped would save him, had burnt holes in his insides, and he was now haemorrhaging internally.

Though the Storms Rage
Yet Will I Dance

The hospital staff told me to call my boys into the hospital. He was not expected to live through the night.

I summoned my boys and rang a friend in Sydney, to contact our American friend. The reply came back. 'I know. God has had me up all night, praying for Kola.'

The nurses were checking Kola's medical readings constantly. Every time, they expected a worse result. Each time, there was an improvement. He went into hospital on the Friday. On Sunday, although still very weak, Kola looked at me,

'I need to speak to Murray. I need to say sorry and I need to forgive.'

With tears in my eyes, I told him I would contact Murray for him. At the gate of death, Kola had finally come to the place where he was ready to put the hurt and bitterness aside.

Monday morning, I brought Kola home and Monday afternoon Murray came around to visit. The door was open. Kola forgave those he needed to, and Murray and he became friends.

The bitterness left Kola and he felt a very deep tangible peace in its place, right through to his death.

Over the next four months, friends would come to visit and comfort him and they would leave, shaking their heads. 'We came to comfort Kola, but we are the ones who were comforted.'

Something else happened on that Monday afternoon when Murray came to visit Kola.

Kola was sitting on a single lounge seat just across from him. They both had their heads bowed and eyes closed as Murray prayed for Kola. Nathan, a friend of Tim's, came to the open front door, then, quickly ran up the hall to Tim's room. Very soon after, both he and Tim came out to us in the lounge room. Nat was very excited as he spoke to Kola.

Chapter 4 – Into the Valley Again
Forgiveness

'You were praying with Murray. Kola, your face was radiant, and you were covered in this brilliant white light.' We all stared at him. This was something totally out of all our experience. We did not know what it was or what it meant. That night we rang our friend in the States and told him what had happened. 'What was it? 'What does it mean?'

Eoin replied, 'This is not the time for me to tell you the full meaning. When the time is right, I will tell you, but this much I will tell. It is the grace of God on Kola.'

One day, four months after Kola had come home from hospital, God gave me two pictures. (Like a dream only this time I was wide awake, going about my chores.)

The first picture was of a crystal jug. The jug held blood and water, separated. An unseen hand picked up the jug and poured its contents out onto the ground.

The second picture was of a tree. The tree had a white slime over its leaves. As I watched, with the sun still shining, a shower of rain fell on the tree, cleansing it, so that its leaves were clean and fresh, wet from the rain and shining in the sunshine.

I again rang Eoin for an interpretation,

'What does it mean? Is Kola going to be healed?'

The answer came back, 'No, Marion, Kola will not be healed. The blood and water were poured out and therefore not available for Kola. In John 19:33,34 the bible speaks of Jesus' death and the piercing of his 'side with a spear, bringing a sudden flow of blood and water'. The separation of blood and water was proof of death. The tree, Marion, represents you. The Holy Spirit will wash over you, immersing you, and bringing healing and restoration.'

Eion continued, 'Marion, now I can give you the full explanation of that radiant white light seen on Kola. When that light is seen, it is an indication that the person, who is surrounded by that light, will soon be taken home. Life on this earth will end, but they are enveloped by the presence of God and are safe for eternity.'

I opened my bible and searched for more confirmation of what I had experienced and been told.

I found what I was looking for in Matthew16:21, where Jesus had just told his disciples he was going to die. Then in Matthew17:1,2 it says:

'After six days, Jesus took with him Peter, James and John... and led them up a high mountain by themselves. There he was transfigured before them. His face shone like the sun, and his clothes became as white as the light.'

It was not long after Jesus was bathed in this light that he entered Jerusalem and died on the cross.

God had prepared me, and I was now ready to let Kola go. Two weeks later, he was gone.

Love Letters

Kola and I met just before Christmas 1973. Kola and his two friends, Jack and Valco were attending a church camp. Between meetings, the three boys were praying together that God would give them a wife. Kola and I met that week. By the end of 1974, all three boys were married.

In February 1974, they came to Tamworth where I lived to take a meeting at my church. Jack and Kola had come to God while in Africa. I had invited them to come to my church and share their story. When Kola returned home, he wrote to me thanking me for inviting them for the weekend. I had billeted them out with church family, but they ate with me, and between meetings we explored Tamworth and the surrounding countryside, talked and enjoyed fellowship together. When they left for home, I knew I had already fallen in love with Kola. He was the only one who wrote to me and our friendship quickly developed into mutual love for each other. I still have all the letters we wrote to each other.

March 11 1974 – Kola wrote:

'Marion, the steps that God may lead us to might or might not be marriage. I hope they do but He is all wise and so let's both of us as God will be faithful, watch our progress and pray continually for His guidance and to see remarkable evidences of His approval of our union."

Our friendship, engagement and our marriage were established on a firm foundation – our relationship to God. When we married, a song was sung, chosen by the both of us. The Chorus reads:

'Each for the other and both for the Lord,

Oh Darling Sweetheart let the angels' record,

Vows sweetly spoken, May they never be broken,

Though the Storms Rage
Yet Will I Dance

Each for the other and both for the Lord.[11]

So long as we maintained our relationship with God, then our relationship with each other stayed strong. Unfortunately, when bitter hurt and disappointment hit us, compounded by grief, we walked away from God. From that day, our relationship with each other weakened until we barely spoke to each other. When we returned to God and came back into relationship with Him, so too was our relationship restored.

April 1 1974 –Here is another excerpt from one of Kola's letters.

'Dearest Marion, I am still praising our Lord for bringing us together. I love Him more dearly because He loves me and has given me a wife who fits my ideas and ideals as revealed in Proverbs 31:10.'

Twenty-five years later, just four months before he died, Kola wrote his last letter to me. I am so blessed to have this letter. I cry every time I read it, but I want to share it because it speaks of total restoration in our relationship and refers back to the letter written 1-4-1974.

9th May – 1999

'Dearest Marion,

25 years ago we met and as our love blossomed I remember quoting Proverbs 31:10 ff. I have just read it again and it is just as true as it was way back then. We have gone through much, ...

Verse 28. Her children arise and call her blessed.

Her <u>husband</u> also and he praises her.'

29. Many women do noble things but you surpass them all.

30. Charm is deceptive; and beauty is fleeting but a woman who fears the Lord is to be praised.

Chapter 4 – Into the Valley Again
Love Letters

I so love seeing you. You are such a strength, to me. I must have been crazy those years ago when my goals were frustrated. But you were right, our boys needed to get an education and friends and wives. It's just we needed to get me something meaningful. But despite this you are my love, my one true love. ... God led us to each other and this wilderness (since 18-1-86 till now) I know that unbelief leads to emptiness.

You have filled me with love (God is love). This love is a refuge to me, ... Marion, you are special, none can compare. My heart is full and satisfied.'

June 1974 – Kola wrote:

'My dearest darling, I love you so much and I don't like being separated from your presence ... the more I think of you and me, the more I want to be with you always.'

May 1999 – Kola wrote a letter, a very tiny letter, barely legible on a scrap of blue paper. Everyone expected him to die that weekend, but he was given another four months. This is what he wrote.

'We still have hope while I live but if not we have the resurrection. Tabitha will be there and whoever else and the rest await the transformation. I am so glad that through the hard times God gave us the strength to stick at it. The alternative is just so horrible. We know we have this Eternal Faith, Hope and Love, Kola.'

This message of hope, Kola wrote about is found in the bible:

1 Thessalonians 4:13–18

Though the Storms Rage
Yet Will I Dance

'Brothers, we do not want you to be ignorant about those who fall asleep, or to grieve like the rest of men who have no hope. We believe that Jesus died and rose again and so we believe that God will bring with Jesus those who have fallen asleep in him. According to the Lord's own word, we tell you that we who are still alive, who are left till the coming of the Lord, will certainly not precede those who have fallen asleep. For the Lord Himself will come down from heaven, with a loud command, with the voice of the archangel and with the trumpet call of God, and the dead in Christ will rise first. After that, we who are still alive and are left will be caught up together with them in the clouds to meet the Lord in the air. And so we will be with the Lord forever.'

Perhaps the greatest love letter of all is written in the bible.

John 3:16

'For God so loved the world that He gave His one and only Son, that whoever believes in him shall not perish but have eternal life.'

Ours is a love story that ultimately will have no end, and Kola's dream 'I want to be with you always' will be a reality.

Saying Goodbye

Kola loved the Australian bush. Pastor Murray led a small service in our garden, set amongst native trees. The Australian wattle and grevillea were in bloom.

I filled the birdbath with grevillea blooms and while birds added their songs, I spoke briefly about Kola's life.

A few days later the boys and I went to the secluded beach Kola had chosen. At sunrise, we scattered his ashes and put flowers on the waves then followed and watched as the tide carried them away and we said goodbye. The morning was cool, and the rising sun tinted the sky and ocean in beautiful rainbow colours. I was glad that Kola's suffering was ended but the separation of death was almost more than we could bear. None of us spoke much. It was as though we were in our own separate cocoons trying to process the moment. Even though we spoke little at that time, nonetheless, we were united in our grief. We slowly walked back to our car and drove home.

Chapter 4 Into the Valley Again ~ For Reflection

1. Are you in a 'valley', a hard time at the moment? Do you know that God not only can, but wants to journey with you?

2. Have you walked away from God? He never walks away from us. Just like the prodigal son, and just like Kola and me, He is calling you back to himself. Can you hear him calling you? Respond to his call. He will never fail you. We still have to walk through the tough times, but we don't have to do it alone.

3. Is there someone you need to reconcile with, someone you need to forgive, or is there some other unresolved issue in your life, which needs dealing with? If there is someone who will not reconcile with you, that is okay. Forgive them and move on. Maybe now is the time to make amends.

4. Read Psalm 23 also known as the Shepherd's Psalm. It gives great comfort.

5. *The Lord is my shepherd. I shall not be in want. He makes me lie down in green pastures. He leads me beside quiet waters. He restores my soul. He guides me in paths of righteousness for his name's sake. Even though I walk through the valley of the shadow of death, I will fear no evil, for you are with me. Your rod and your staff, they comfort me. You prepare a table before me in the presence of my enemies.*

6. *You anoint my head with oil; my cup overflows. Surely goodness and love will follow me all the days of my life, and I will dwell in the house of the Lord forever.*

Chapter 5 – What the Locusts Have Eaten

1. What the Locusts Have Eaten
2. Gaining Through Losing
3. Home Again
4. Crossing Over
5. February 13
6. Lionel
7. Are You Willing?
8. Door of Hope Garden
9. Amazing Grace – I've Been Set Free
10. Puppies and Purple Tibouchinas
11. A Bunch of Nasturtiums
12. Epilogue

What the Locusts have Eaten

"I will repay you for the years the locusts have eaten."

Joel 2:25

Over the years I have lost much, but God has given me a promise. 'I will repay you for the years the locusts have eaten.' Over those same years I have seen how God has been at work, miraculously restoring those things which were taken from me. This chapter is not about loss, but about restoration and a God who truly loves me and walks beside me.

Gaining Through Losing

Four months after Kola's death I had an experience which showed me that even in the midst of loss there is also gain. Here is my journal entry from 19 January 2000:

> Early in the morning while I slept, I dreamt of Kola. He was well and we were visiting a Ukrainian family. He was lying on a sofa and I bent over, kissed him and told him I loved him. I then embraced and hugged him tightly. I seemed to be hugging him tighter and tighter, until I woke up and found myself hugging my own body.
>
> I was completely broken. I sobbed, huge, wrenching sobs as I awoke to the reality of being alone. My dream had been so real, that the parting was as painful as the day I had hugged him and said goodbye at the hospital four months earlier.
>
> Yesterday had been his birthday, but I had assigned certain jobs to be done, kept myself busy and got through the day. In the waking- moments, no such luxury was afforded me and my thoughts were free to take me where they wanted.
>
> Again, as so often when I awake after a dream, I reach for my bible or a book I am reading at that time. I reached for my book and read,
>
>> 'Dear Evelyn, I am really going to watch for your next book, . . . Gaining Through Losing – I gained through losing my husband. . . . he was fatally injured by his chain saw. It's a long story how the Lord used Ron's death to bring us all back to California, and how, one by one, each of us came to Him. Eternal fruit!
>>
>> Gained, . . . the privilege of being one of the branches God chooses to prune – so that I can realize my full potential of what I can be – so that I can bear eternal fruit!

Though the Storms Rage
Yet Will I Dance

But though He causes grief, yet will He have compassion according to the multitude of His mercies. For He doth not afflict willingly (Lam 3: 32-33), But his pruning is always to develop our full potential.'[lll]

These words sunk into my mind, although I was still hurting too much to really appreciate them.

Not long after, my friend Jackie rang me from work. I told her what had happened and of this new wave of grief enveloping me.

What she said next just totally astounded me. 'Marion, what you had with Kola was very special, but try not to think of your loss, but what you've gained.'

Gaining through losing! In awe, I asked her, 'Why did you say that?'

'I don't know,' she replied.

'Have you recently read anything on loss and gain?' I queried.

'No.'

'I want to read you something.' I picked up the book and read out the above passage to her. We were both in awe, at how God communicates both to and through us.

Home Again

We'd sold our home in 1988 before we set off on our journey around Australia. A caravan was our home for the next five years, followed by rental properties for another six years. We looked at several places, but did not buy any. In May 1999, Kola and I drove past a lovely home set amongst trees, which he thought we should purchase. We didn't do any more concerning the house, because Kola's health rapidly declined, and he died four months later.

After the funeral, I told my sons that I wanted to buy our own home. The three of them got in their car and went house hunting. They soon returned, their words tumbling over each other as they spoke.

'Mum, we've found the perfect house for us.'

'Five bedrooms – one for each of us, and a studio for you.'

'Four-car lock-up accommodation – We've four cars!'

'It's set amongst trees, next to a gully, on an acre of land. Mum you can have a great garden.'

'And it has a creek and a gully with water dragons diving into the water.'

Well, I just had to see it. We all piled into Tim's car and off we went.

As we pulled up outside this house, I just stared at it. It was the house Kola had shown me four months earlier.

That week I entered into a contract for the house. I paid cash for it. No mortgage. It was ours. It was perfect.

Two months passed before we were able to move in, as the previous owners needed to find another property to move into. The two

Though the Storms Rage
Yet Will I Dance

months passed quickly, as we cleaned our rental home and packed our belongings. I did five tax forms. At that time, we did our own, so I did one for Kola, even though he had died, one for me and one for each of the three boys.

Sometime during those two months, while doing the housework, I saw two scenes, like in a dream except I was fully awake. I wrote them down. I had been getting dreams for a year now so was getting used to having them, but I still did not always know what they meant. The two scenes I saw were these:

A pine branch of dark green leaves, tipped at the end of the branch with new lime green leaves, shone in the sunlight. As I looked at it, a cloud passed over cloaking the scene in shade.

The second vision was of a waterhole that had tiny yellow water lilies resting on the surface of the still water. Again, the scene changed as I watched. Muddy floodwater filled the gully to the brim, before quickly receding. I asked a friend what they meant. This was his answer.

'Marion, you have been very busy, and you have not grieved fully, so you are going to have a period of depression. It will not be deep and will be very brief.'

He was right. I had been very busy, and did not have time to process my grief. Even the day after Kola died, I spent three hours counselling two women with their problems.

We moved into our home at the end of November. It was summer and in the early morning I would take my bible and sit at the table on my back veranda.

I looked out towards the gully and the tall bunya pines, which grew along the bank. A light rain had fallen during the night and raindrops glistened on the leaves. New lime-green leaves tipped the end of branches of dark green leaves. The rays of the early morning sun touched the top branches and they shone. I stared at one particular branch high up in the

Chapter 5 – What the Locusts Have Eaten
Home Again

tree and recognised it as the one I had seen weeks earlier. As I looked at it in wonder, I knew that God had chosen and kept this house for us.

Our home became our refuge not only for the four of us, but for many people over the years. I still live here.

Crossing Over

It was now eleven months since Kola had passed away. Tim was travelling into Brisbane to film an art exhibition/festival for a colleague of his. I decided to go with him and got him to drop me off at the Botanical Gardens. It was a beautiful day, and the gardens were at their peak. After looking around for a while, I decided to visit the Japanese Gardens. It was early spring and the azaleas there would be in full bloom. Kola and I had often visited the Botanical Gardens and especially loved the Japanese Gardens. This was the first time I had visited them since losing Kola.

Before leaving home that morning I had read in my bible, the account of the time when Elijah was taken up to heaven and Elisha was left alone (2Kings 2:6-12). Up until this time, Elisha had stayed close by his master's side. On the bank of the Jordan River, Elijah had struck the water, the waters of the river had divided and the two of them had crossed over on dry ground.

After Elijah had been taken to heaven and Elisha was now alone, he tore his clothes and grieved for his master.

Now the time had come for Elisha to re-cross the Jordan. Picking up Elijah's coat which had fallen from him, Elisha turned and went again to the bank of the Jordan. Whether he wanted to or not, it was time for Elisha to move into the next part of his life. It was time for him to test what he had learnt while he had been with Elijah. Striking the water with the cloak in his hand, the waters parted, and he re-crossed the Jordan alone.

A section of the Japanese Gardens featured a waterfall, which fell into a pond and continued to flow in a small gurgling brook that could be crossed via three stepping-stones. I remember doing this with Kola and taking photos there.

Though the Storms Rage
Yet Will I Dance

Now I was alone, and I realised that my reading of this morning was about to be played out in my own life. Now I too must cross over my 'Jordan,' that small stream. Like Elisha crossing over without Elijah and moving into the next section of his life, so too must I. Realising the full impetus of this symbolic act, I stepped onto the first stepping-stone. I was truly alone. There was no one else there. I began sobbing, heart-wrenching sobs that tore at me, but I knew I must cross over. I was on a threshold. I stepped onto the second stone, and then the third. Nearby was a garden seat. I sat down, looking back to where I had just crossed over.

I did not know this was going to be part of my day when I chose to visit the gardens. But God knew and He prepared me for what I had to do.

Those few steps had been vital. It really was a crossing-over in my life. Yes, it was hard, but God went ahead. He prepared the way, He prepared me, and He walked with me. He always does.

Moving from being part of a couple to being single is never just one step. Death, divorce or separation gives a defining line between marriage and singleness, between being part of a couple and dancing solo. However, the transition is made over a series of steps. For me, the transition began when Kola was still with me.

The first step was when Kola was diagnosed with cancer and we knew it was terminal. We were given four-and-a-half-years to prepare. While all the time praying and believing for healing, we still had to face the possibility, indeed the probability, that Kola would die.

The next and hardest step was the day he died. Then followed the packing away of his clothes, the funeral, and all the firsts – the first wedding anniversary just three weeks after he died, the first Christmas and so on through the first year.

These were all part of saying goodbye, but becoming single again also held many hellos. There were many new and exciting challenges and experiences such as returning to work, buying our new house, my first overseas trip, and many more. Crossing over embraces all of these.

Chapter 5 – What the Locusts Have Eaten
Crossing Over

Crossing over that small stream that day was symbolic of the great change in my life that I was embarking on. It was not by choice, but has been and still is an exciting adventure.

Lionel

My brother Lionel is twenty years older than me. While I was still only a baby, Lionel got married to Joyce and left home. Almost from birth I had been cared for by other people in other homes. Lionel was virtually a stranger to me.

Early in March 2009, I had a dream in which I was given a sepia photo of my family, including myself when I was a baby.

I was sixty-two at the time of this dream. I had never seen a photo of myself as a baby. Although I had met them, I did not really know my brother and his wife or children. When I turned nineteen, I discovered who my mother was, and travelled to Nowra, New South Wales to reconnect with my sister. It was a very special time. However, returning to Tamworth where I lived, anger set in because of what had happened. My dad and stepmum had sworn everyone to secrecy regarding my true mother.

'If all my family had lied to me for nineteen years, then who needs a family.'

I wiped my brother, sister and parents from my life and set out on a path of independence. They had abandoned me, so now I would abandon them. I didn't need them.

Now at sixty-two, more than forty years later, this dream awakened in me a need to reconnect with my brother.

When I arrived at Adelaide Airport, Lionel was waiting for me. My emotions were so mixed. Excitement at getting to know him intermingled with a lot of apprehension. After all, I didn't know this brother of mine. Tears escaped from my eyes as we embraced, probably for the first time in our lives. Blended in with all the other emotions coursing through me was the emotion of sadness. Sadness that it had taken more than sixty years, sixty lost years, to reach this point in our lives.

Though the Storms Rage
Yet Will I Dance

Over the next four days we caught up with those lost years of our lives as we explored parts of Adelaide, the Barossa Valley where a lot of fine wines are produced and the Adelaide Hills. Lionel put on his GPS in the car and religiously followed every instruction. We passed a sign saying 17km to Adelaide.

Joyce pointed to it, 'Follow that sign.' But Lionel was glued to the GPS. I think we explored every dirt road and goat track in the hills. Sometime later, I pointed to the same sign. 'Lionel, follow that sign. It is only seventeen kilometres– less than half an hour home.' But no, we followed the GPS and arrived home three hours later.

The next day my niece Vicki, their youngest daughter, called in and took me to her beautiful home. We talked about the lost years and where we left off. We hugged and talked, and reconciliation took place.

Later the next day, Toni, their oldest daughter rang and again reconciliation occurred.

On the Sunday, their son Clinton and his partner came over. I remembered Clinton from when I got married. I loved him back then, even though our meeting was brief, and I loved him just as much when he walked into his dad's home. I threw my arms around him and around Brenton, his partner, hugging them both. My affection for them was spontaneous and real.

I looked at my brother, who was sitting at the dining room table crying. I sat down opposite and reached out to him. He raised his eyes to me. 'I am so sorry. Sorry that I didn't do anything to keep you in the family.'

The simple act of hugging his beautiful, kind, gentle, gay son and his partner had broken down a barrier. Everyone went about whatever they were doing, and Lionel and I talked about our childhoods, how we had both grown up without a mother, siblings and the loving protection and companionship of a father who was present to our emotional need.

Chapter 5 – What the Locusts Have Eaten
Lionel

Two of Lionel's main interests and skills are photography and collecting and collating historical facts and figures. He showed me many family photos which I had not seen and printed copies for me of the ones I liked. Amongst these photos, was a sepia photo of our family when I was a baby- my mother and father, my sister and brother and me.

February 13

Our precious daughter, Tabitha was born on 13 February 1977. Yet we had to say goodbye to her the day before her second birthday.

Hands clasping a single pink rosebud, she lay like a beautiful wax doll on her hospital bed. She was dressed in a white nightdress, which was scalloped at the neckline, with cotton wool at her throat betraying the fact that she had just undergone heart surgery. Her soft, honey brown hair was combed, framing her little face and her eyes were closed in the sleep of death.

Time moved on as we adapted to life without Tabitha. Over the years we watched our precious children Timothy, Jonathon and Luke grow to adulthood. While I revelled and rejoiced over my boys' many pursuits and achievements, I often thought of my little girl and what death had robbed me of. I did not have the joy of watching her grow. Neither did I have the experience of doing those special mother-daughter things.

After my husband passed away, however, God began a miraculous series of events in my life. I may have missed my own daughter's milestones, but God blessed me with many surrogate daughters. He was indeed restoring 'the years that the locusts had eaten'.

KELSEY, sitting at the piano, turned to me as I was about to begin her lesson. 'Marion, will you come to my house for drinks and nibbles and be with me while I get ready for my formal and graduation from high school. It will just be my family and close friends. Please come.'

She was so beautiful in her long formal dress, her hair specially done and wearing a corsage which I'd made for her. I went to Kelsey's formal, followed by her 21st birthday, her engagement and her wedding.

'Marion, Stewie and I would like you to play for our wedding. Will you play for us, please?'

Though the Storms Rage
Yet Will I Dance

I played for their wedding on a crisp morning on top of the mountain range, under a huge camphor laurel tree in her grandmother's backyard. As they were presented as Mr And Mrs, I played a piece I'd written especially for them, *Winter Wedding*.

A guest asked Kelsey's Mum, 'Who is that person, playing the piano?'

Her mum replied, 'She's Kelsey's music teacher. Oh no, that is not quite right, she's family!' I was given a corsage to wear, and for Christmas, Kelsey and Stewie gave me a wedding photo book, with photos selected just for me.

SARAH's mum had been my best friend, but five years after my husband's death, she also passed away. Shortly after Sarah had lost her mum, she completed a double degree in medicine and surgery.

One evening, Sarah rang. 'Marion, my graduation from medicine is soon. Will you join my family for my graduation?'

I knew that seating at graduation ceremonies was limited, as I'd already attended the graduations of my sons. What an extraordinary privilege and honour. I was as proud of her as I would have been of my own daughter.

EMMA, Sarah's older sister, called me next. 'Marion, Scott has just proposed to me. We're talking wedding plans. Come over.'

'Emma, I'm in bed!'

'Get out of bed, please come over.' And so, I found myself amidst the excitement of wedding plans.

The wedding was to be held in a vineyard in the Hunter Valley of New South Wales. Several villas had been booked.

'Marion, I'm putting you in with Dad, my brother, aunty and uncle, my bridesmaids and me.'

Chapter 5 – What the Locusts Have Eaten
February 13

Oh, my! I'm not part of the family, but she had put me in with them. I spent the night there. I watched Emma and her bridesmaids have their hair and makeup done and get dressed. I looked on as the pre-wedding photos were taken and took some myself. I saw the flowers arrive and ironed her father's shirt. I was part of the pre-wedding nerves and preparations. What I thought could never be mine was given me as a very precious gift.

RACHEL, my son Tim's wife, looked at me; 'I want you to teach me for my Associate Diploma in piano performance.'

I stared at her. Would my being her piano teacher put too much pressure on our very new relationship? I was very apprehensive about this request, but I said yes. None of my sons had followed music as a career. Would my daughter have taken up music? I will never know, but here was Rachel, my daughter-in-law, wanting me to teach her.

She gained her associate Diploma of Music (piano performing) following it up with her Diploma of Teaching (piano), gaining the second highest mark in Australia for that year. As we worked through hours of intense study, a deep bond developed between us and I was able to pass on my mantle of music, my knowledge and experience to her.

KYLIE, my second daughter-in-law-to-be, looked at me expectantly, 'I'm going for a fitting for my wedding dress. Would you like to come with me?'

'Yes, I'd love to.' I inwardly marvelled yet again at the great favour being given me, as I added yet another mother-daughter experience to my growing list.

Kylie also offered me perhaps the greatest offer a mother can be given. Would I, along with her husband Luke, and her own mother, be with her for the birth of her first child?

'Restoring what the locust has eaten?' Oh, surely so. I felt that my cup of joy was flowing over, yet more was to be poured in.

Though the Storms Rage
Yet Will I Dance

KAIJA, a young girl from my church, needed somewhere to live. Her parents' home was up on the range, too distant and too dangerous a drive for her to be negotiating every day. She lived with me for six months before moving into her own flat. Before she left, Kaija asked, 'Can I get married from your place?'

Wow! I could hardly believe what I was being asked.

The day before the wedding arrived and Kaija and her three bridesmaids moved in, along with dresses, shoes, makeup, chatter, nerves and lots of fun and laughter.

Very early the next morning, I needed to take my little dog outside. Returning along the hallway to my bedroom I was met by a very wide-awake Kaija.

'Well, you're not going back to sleep, are you?' She shook her head.

'Hot chocolate and my bed?' This time she nodded shyly, and we were soon tucked up in my bed with hot chocolate and photo albums of my recent trip to the U.K.

What a special time. Here was a mother-daughter experience, which in all my imaginings, I could never have envisaged.

Later, as we stood in the dining room, I looked at the calendar hanging on the wall by my phone. I gasped as I saw the date and realised the special significance of this day. It was not only Kaija's wedding day, but my daughter's birthday, February 13.

Are You Willing?

4.00 A.M. I couldn't stay in bed any longer. The pain in my neck and lower back is gnawingly sore and I cannot bear the pillow. I can't bear no pillow either or the thin hard mattress.

Thus read my journal entry of the 9 February 2011. A team of us from my church were en-route to Dipalog on the island of Mindanao in the Philippines. We had spent that first night in a hotel at Manila, the capital of the Philippines.

Flying into Dipalog was so beautiful. The small plane landed on an airstrip built along the beach. We came in to land with the sandy beach and the blue water stretching out to our right. To our left was the equatorial green of coconut trees and other lush growth with small grass-roofed buildings dotted throughout. Tall rugged mountains formed the backdrop.

We were there for a conference, a training session for pastors and workers, a time for healing and equipping for these wonderful, gentle people. While I had really wanted to be there and to participate, the pain became an overriding force. My journal entry of 11 February- 2011 says,

I am experiencing a lot of pain– either pain or struggling to stay awake because of the effect of the painkillers. People are excited with what is happening. I can't enter into it all fully because I'm hurting too much.

On the Saturday afternoon, we went to a very poor village on the banks of the Dipalog River. The ground was damp and there were crabholes in the mud.

The houses were built of bamboo, thatch, reed matting and rusted corrugated iron. They were tiny houses, built off the ground on stilts because the high tides wash up and flow beneath their houses. During flood times their houses would be swamped with water or washed away altogether. They had no screens on their windows and the walls were not sealed from mosquitoes. The living was basic.

Children came to the meeting, beautiful children with big dark eyes, shining black hair and spotlessly clean clothes. Mums and grandmas came, and some men stood in the background.

One striking man, shirtless and with long wavy black hair, arrived with his small child of about eighteen months old. A battle was raging inside of him: to be here or not to be. He came and he went, once on a tricycle, taking his child with him. But he came back, drawn to the message being given.

We began our meeting by singing and dancing with the children. There was such joy, as Nicole led them in songs of Jesus. We handed out lollies, drinks, soft fluffy toys and balloons twisted into various shapes. The children thronged to the givers, holding out hands, reaching eagerly for their gifts, drinks and food.

The children's ministry flowed into a healing crusade. Charles (our Pastor) spoke of salvation, of healing, of his own background—a black man fathered by an abusive alcoholic stepfather, and how he came to find the healing love of his Father God. Using a microphone and amplifier he spoke to the unseen people still in their homes.

Pastor Gill, the Filipino pastor, interpreted and the message of love went out, penetrating the thin and incomplete walls of the many small homes clustered in that small riverbed village. Many were healed—a painful shoulder, headache, blindness. When a small girl was asked if we could pray for her, she said 'Grandma' (in her own dialect). She led us to her home where we found the grandmother who suffered from double vision. After prayer, her double vision went, and she could once more see clearly. The shirtless, long-haired man also allowed Charles to pray for him.

In my journal on the Sunday, I wrote,

Chapter 5 – What the Locusts Have Eaten
Are You Willing?

I have prayed for people and they have been healed, and yet my pain remains. I have had healing before – the nerves to the big toe of my left foot restored, osteoporosis removed, and my shoulder healed, and yet I struggle with this. I have decided to just surrender it to God and learn to live with it until such time as God heals me.

During the course of eighteen months the pain got worse and spread throughout my entire body, except for my hands and fingers. It would take me twenty minutes to roll over in bed in order to get up and go to the toilet.

I could only walk with the aid of a walking stick and then only in a shuffle putting about a toe's length in front of the other foot. Standing, sitting, lying down, walking – everything was a struggle filled with pain.

Different people said things, such as,

'You've opened a door to allow Satan in. You need to find out what it is and repent of it.'

'You don't have enough faith to receive a healing,' and other such comments.

I went to many different medical people, seeking answers. 'What was wrong with me?' and 'What can I do to get better?' I searched my heart and my life to see if there was indeed something I had done, or maybe something I needed to do. Then I went to a doctor who diagnosed me as having polymyalgia, an autoimmune disease, which gained entrance when I had a viral infection and a fever. I went home and googled it on my laptop. It made sense. The normal treatment is cortisone. My doctor didn't want me on cortisone, so instead I alternated anti-inflammatory medication with a strong painkiller.

Four months later, two things happened. Pastor Charles came up to me during worship, put his hand on my shoulder and said, 'God is very proud of you, and He is showing you off. Just as he said, "Hey Satan, did you consider my servant Job," so he is doing the same to you.' My reaction was one of awe and relief. God was allowing this to happen to me. It was nothing I did or did not do.

At about the same time, God gave me a dream in which He asked, 'Are you willing to go where I send you and to do what I ask of you, despite the pain?'

I had endured this pain for thirteen months at that time and I answered God, 'No, it is too hard.'

God then asked me, a second time, 'Are you willing to go where I send you and to do what I ask of you, despite the pain?' He then added, 'I walked the Gethsemane Road'. That undid me, and I replied, 'Yes, I will go, and I will do whatever you ask of me'.

From that point on I had peace, a deep peace which was unshakeable, whatever was said to me. The pain continued for another five months but began to lessen, until finally it was gone.

Door of Hope Garden

When I was experiencing the crippling effects of polymyalgia, it was impossible to take care of my garden. Little by little I let things go. The vines and weeds rapidly took control. I stood on my balcony looking over my garden and wept. I loved my home and my garden, but I would have to sell if this crippled painful state continued.

To sell my home meant I would have to prepare my house and yard for sale, which of course was for me at that time, impossible.

Towards the end of the eighteen months that I had polymyalgia, the pain lessened gradually, and I began to get my mobility back. Once again, I stood on my balcony and looked across my garden. I saw the gully and the waterhole, the Bunya pines standing majestically along the gully, the forest clearing which was my yard, the stand of Radiata pines down along the creek, and the creek itself. I looked at my large Camphor Laurel tree and the staghorns and crow's nest, which were growing so happily in its branches.

I spoke softly, 'God you gave me this house and garden, now I must give it back to you'. Within days of giving my house and garden back to God an amazing transformation of my garden began.

I had fairly new neighbours, Des and Jenny across the gully. Not long after they moved in, we had a flood.

The gully raged and broke its banks across the street, pouring across the road and down the gully between us. At the same time the creek at the back rose higher and higher. This rise coincided with a king tide, which pushed the water backwards. The Caboolture River pushed the water back into Warraba Creek, which in turn pushed its overload into our creek until the creek flowed backwards and both gully and creek spilled its muddy contents onto both my neighbour's and my land. While my yard went under, my house and shed were above flood level. My neighbour was not so fortunate. The raging water in the gully washed very close to the foundations of their home, while the overflow from the creek covered not just their yard but inundated the bottom level of their home and also their shed.

When the water went down, and everything was put back in order, Des contacted the council and asked to have the water from the gully piped underground. Des came to me and asked if he could build a retaining wall along my side of the gully. I told him I didn't have that kind of money.

'Marion, all I want is your permission.'

Over the next few months, the gully water was piped underground to a newly built dam just below our homes. Des then fenced the dam and piped the overflow from the dam underground all the way to the creek.

He built a beautiful retaining wall, and steps with railings. Most of the wall is on my property and cost thousands of dollars but it cost me nothing. Benches were placed in strategic places along the wall under the shady trees. Des brought home a discarded, large play gym from his work and installed it in our shared space. The council filled in above the pipes, covering them with topsoil and turf. Des backfilled along the retaining wall. Jenny and I then planted our gardens, using the same plants along the wall, which wrapped around the front and into Jenny's yard.

During this time, I attended a meeting with a friend at a 'Quiet Garden'. The garden provided areas where people could come and sit quietly, taking time to reflect and find peace in the midst of the busyness and often turmoil of their lives. That garden inspired me to make my garden into a 'quiet' garden. I collected outdoor tables and chairs and created several nooks where people could sit quietly without distraction.

My garden held so many stories of restoration and hope. I gave names to the different sections of garden, then wrote a story or poem for each location, illustrating and laminating each poster.

Chapter 5 – What the Locusts Have Eaten
Door of Hope Garden

My Victory Garden is a wide area framing my driveway and wrapping around to border part of the footpath at the front of my house. It is home to many small, flowering trees and shrubs, palms and pencil pines. Orchids and begonias grow in pots in the centre of the golden canes. Several large pots containing lovely yellow and white candle-bushes were placed along the driveway. Bromiliads and other low-growing plants provided groundcover and yellow and green ribbon grass provide a border around the edge of the garden. A birdbath featured in the front portion of the garden.

An old electricity meter box painted red and planted with flowers tells the story of the day it ignited due to fraudulent and faulty work by a dishonest electrician. Along with the story, I have the text 'I will give you ... beauty for ashes, the oil of joy for mourning, the garment of praise for the spirit of heaviness. Isaiah 61:3'.

To its right, between my mandarin and orange tree, is a statue of three puppies holding a 'welcome' sign. The story of 'Sparky', my little dog is also there. It is his burial place. I hope that this place may provide a door for someone to process some part of their grief.

Down in the left-hand corner of my garden is an old kayak also painted red and planted with flowers. It too has its own story to tell.

Behind the shed, beneath the mango tree is a table and two chairs. Hanging plants adorn the branches of the tree. I call this corner, 'The Hiding Place'. I have written a three-stanza poem for this area. The last verse says:

'In the cool of the evening the spicy scent

Drifts up from my verdant stream

While the wildlife sing their evensong

This is a place to dream.

Though the Storms Rage
Yet Will I Dance

He hideth my soul in the cleft of the rock

Says the words of that old, old song

Let him give you rest and a hiding place

To run to, your whole life long.'^{IV}

About three years after a runaway car destroyed my front garden, it again became a disaster zone. The entire garden from the mailbox down to the house and along the footpath had been razed by a scrub turkey who thought it would be a great source of building materials for its nest. The roots of all the palms were exposed. The bromeliads, hippeastrums and other plants were now either non-existent or shredded remnants of plants. All the pots along the driveway were empty, with plants now destroyed, lying on the ground. All of the plants, mulch and soil were now heaped into a large mound for the turkey's new nest. I had tried everything to distract it and save my garden, but nothing had worked.

Eventually I contacted wildlife services and paid $190 to have the turkey trapped and removed. Three hours later, a second male turkey took over from the first turkey. This one was even more destructive, and it cost another $80 to have it removed.

Turkeys mate and nest during August till November, coinciding with our leaf-fall season. 'Place furniture where the mound was', I was instructed. I raked the mound back across my garden, gathered barrowloads of leaf-mulch, pavers and garden furniture and reclaimed my garden. Gathering up my tattered shrubs, I pruned them hard, refilled the tubs with potting mix and replanted them. Wire netting which I'd laid down over all of my front garden in an effort to deter the turkey was rolled up and stored.

My garden now looks lovely, and that is why I call it my 'Victory' Garden.

Chapter 5 – What the Locusts Have Eaten
Door of Hope Garden

Our gardens and our homes are places where people can come and move from hopelessness into hope, from devastation to victory, from grief to peace and joy.

One day, after our gardens were restored, my pastors came, along with a lot of friends, and our properties were dedicated as joint 'Door of Hope' gardens. Many people have gained hope, health and healing over the years as they have passed through both of our homes. I also have received healing in different areas of my life.

Amazing Grace
I've Been Set Free

I gave my first full piano recital when I was sixty-five. The beautiful hymn *Amazing Grace* opened the recital. The melody is an old Negro tune, which John Newton first heard coming from the belly of the slave ship he captained en-route to England. It changed him and he wrote the words of the hymn to that melody:

Amazing Grace! How sweet the sound,

That saved a wretch like me.

I once was lost but now am found;

Was blind but now I see. [v]

The arrangement of *Amazing Grace* was one I had developed at school. I was teaching piano students who needed sacred music to play as one of the requirements of piano competitions with other schools. I didn't have anything suitable for my students who were studying Grade 6 and 7 Piano, so I adapted *Amazing Grace* for them. I wrote it in the form of a theme and four variations with an introduction and an ending. This piece then became the first item of my recital and the theme for the whole recital.

Why was I sixty-five before I presented this recital?

The abuse and lies told to me throughout my childhood had effectively crippled me from becoming the person I was born to be.

Although music was in me, I was not allowed to learn to play the piano until I was eleven, when Dad finally gave in and let me have piano lessons. Until then, I had taught myself to play the piano. I played in concerts from then on, but only one or two pieces and I was always an absolute bundle of nerves because I believed I really was no good at anything. I also believed I was ugly. Looking back at photos of myself, I know now that I was actually a very attractive looking child and young person. I was wearing the lies which had been hurled at me. I remember Kola saying to me regularly, 'You've got your stepmother on your shoulder. Brush her off!'

In early, 2012 I attended an International Leaders School of Ministry. During one session, they talked about the effect of lies spoken to us and over our lives. As they spoke, I knew that I needed healing in this area of life. I needed to be free from the power that those lies have had, and still had over my life. I stood for prayer. As the speaker broke off the power of those lies on my life, I knew that I was free. It was as though a big weighty sack had been lifted off of me.

The following week at my women's group, I shared with them what had happened. One of the women, Shirley, looked at me, and said, 'We need another recital!' Over the past few years, I had given recitals of my diploma students.

'Of my students?' I queried.

'No. You.'

'Yes, okay, I will do it.'

The die was cast. I began preparing for the recital.

I asked Shirley and her husband Bob if they would sing two brackets of songs. I asked another friend to give an item and I asked a student to play a Chopin Waltz. The rest of the recital was me. In the past, I would never have done this, but 'me' now was a different person. I prepared eight pieces.

Chapter 5 – What the Locusts Have Eaten
Amazing Grace
I've Been Set Free

Before playing each piece in the recital, I gave a little more of my story. I finished with a YouTube presentation of Amazing Grace, sung by a Negro man who also gave us the story of how this song came into being.

The recital was finished. I had not been nervous, but loved giving the presentation. Although I played a couple of classical pieces, most of my presentation consisted of variations on old hymns, which I had arranged.

The next day was Sunday. As I sat in church, voices all around me were raised in worship, yet I was hearing a very different melody. It replayed in my head, and when church was over, I left for home immediately. Sitting at my piano, I played the song I had been hearing and wrote the piece out onto music manuscript. This was my first original composition. I played the piece over the phone to my friend, Eileen, and she said:

'I know what you must name it – Tabitha's Song.'

I thought of what I had just played, and of my little girl who had died many years earlier, and agreed.

'Yes, it suits her.'

My first original piece was a gift, a download from God, named for my precious daughter. Over the next few weeks more compositions were given to me. Within two months I had seven original pieces and five arrangements.

I began using them for my students, although many of them were worship songs. One night I had a call from Glen, a friend who was in the process of rewriting some of the syllabi for the Australian Guild of Music Syllabus. Glen had examined some of my students and had heard a few of my pieces.

'Marion, I would like to list your pieces in the Light Classical Recital Syllabus.'

'A lot of them are worship songs.'

Though the Storms Rage
Yet Will I Dance

'That's okay, I want you to list them all, write out their names and the grade and email the list to me tonight.'

After speaking to Glen, I sat and reflected on what was happening. None of these things had been in my thinking at all.

'If they are to be listed, then I will need to get hard copies!' I published two volumes of sheet music. Tim, my oldest son, designed the covers. I named my music *Reflections Volume 1*, and *Reflections Volume 2*. As a companion to these, I recorded a CD of all twelve pieces.

I am still composing more pieces. Amazing grace! I have indeed been set free.

Puppies and Purple Tibouchinas

God also used the pets we had over the years to bring healing and restoration into my life.

We had made our choice. As we moved towards the stairs of the house, all the puppies except one resumed playing. The one puppy followed us to the foot of the stairs, then sat and waited for our return. How did he know that we had chosen him, or maybe had he also chosen us?

Laddie was a tricolour collie rough, just like Lassie of TV fame. Only six weeks old, he settled with us immediately. He knew he was ours, and we, all five of us, were his.

When we let our chooks out for a run and a scratch around the yard, he made it his responsibility to protect them. He would shepherd them into one corner of the yard and sit and watch them. If an errant chook decided to stray, Laddie would quickly guide it back to whatever part of the yard he had chosen for them to be in. He was, however, gentleness personified and never hurt any of them.

We brought him home in 1985. When we sold our home in 1988, hooked up our caravan and set off around Australia, Laddie came with us. He joined us on most of our excursions. By day he travelled in the car with us and at night he slept on his bed in the caravan so that we knew he was safe.

Because I was teaching fulltime when we got him, and during our trip I was also away a lot, teaching in different schools around Australia, Kola was his primary carer. We loved him and he loved us.

By 1999, Laddie was fourteen years old and showing the signs of age, which we knew would inevitably take him from us.

Though the Storms Rage
Yet Will I Dance

Kola was very sick and in hospital. His hair was all falling out from his chemotherapy treatment. He had collected his hair, put it in a bag and asked me to bury it with Laddie when he died. That day came in May. Laddie was having a lot of trouble walking and he'd also become incontinent. Tim came with me to the vet, where my best friend Lorna joined us. We held him and talked to him as the vet put him to sleep. Jonathon and Luke meanwhile dug the grave. We buried him and planted a Tibouchina, a small subtropical tree with masses of purple flowers in summer and autumn. The Tibouchina was also Kola's request, for it was his favourite tree and they were still in flower at this time. That afternoon I drove into Brisbane to be with Kola who was in hospital.

In September, we said goodbye to Kola and in November moved into our own home. I planted a Tibouchina in the front garden for Kola. Soon after, I bought a guinea pig, then another guinea pig, and the next year I brought home a puppy, a tiny fluffy scrap of energy, half Chihuahua, half Pomeranian. I called him Sparky.

We had him for fourteen years. When he died, I wrote the following story about him:

SPARKY

Shredded paper flew in all directions and in the midst of the mayhem was a tiny puppy, small enough to fit in the palm of my hand. The only pup remaining of the litter, his actions spoke volumes. 'My world may have changed, my mother and my siblings gone, but I am in control of my world.'

I had just lost my husband and father to my three sons. This puppy displayed the characteristics I needed for this new season of my life.

Sparky he was named and Sparky he was in character. He was my constant companion for 14 years.

Chapter 5 – What the Locusts Have Eaten
Puppies and Purple Tibouchinas

Thick clouds had been building all afternoon, with the distant thunder rolling in closer and louder, until just after 5.00 pm on the 6th January, 2014, the first heavy drops of rain began to fall, the lightning rent the sky, and the storm began just as my Sparky closed his deep black eyes in the sleep of death. He was gone.

As Luke, my son, and I buried him, just as the sun was beginning to set, the storm was at its fiercest. Forked lightning zig-zagged to earth followed immediately on its heels by the deafening booms of the thunder.

As Luke dug the grave, I held Sparky, ducking first to the right and then to the left, away from the darts of lightning which were striking all around us.

'Is it deep enough?'

'No, not yet.'

'Luke, is that handle wooden or metal?'

'Metal, Mum.'

'Oh, my goodness, I'll be putting you in the hole instead of Sparky.'

Finally the hole was deep enough and we quickly placed Sparky in the grave and both of us now with a spade, filled the hole.

'Quickly, put the birdbath on top.'

Luke placed the birdbath and shouted, 'Let's get out of here'. Then, soaked to the skin, we raced toward the house.

The storm soon passed over and the sky turned a brilliant red, colouring the house, the shrubs and the lawn into iridescent crimson. The pine trees behind the grave stood silhouetted black against the fiery sky.

Sparky's burial matched his character, his name and his life. No greater tribute could he have had.

....

Though the Storms Rage
Yet Will I Dance

I still had another little dog who I'd bought six months after getting Sparky. I had seen her on the Saturday. She was a tiny Maltese/miniature fox-terrier cross. Her coat was mainly white with caramel patches and her ears looked as though she had brushed her ears in cinders.

On the Sunday, Jonathon and I had spent the day cleaning gutters and putting out a bushfire, which had come dangerously close to our friend Lorna's place.

Neighbours, many of them unknown, came to our aid with rags or mats, which we dipped into the pool and then used to swat the spot fires, which were breaking out. Others had buckets, rakes, brooms, whatever they could grab, to stop the fire reaching the house.

We would extinguish a pat of cow manure and go to the next, only to find that the dried-out cow manure would reignite as soon as we turned our backs. Eventually the fire brigade arrived, and the fire was brought under control.

Another friend was evacuated from her home on the same day, and the Elimbah School, about ten minutes away, also had a very close brush with the fire when leaves in the gutter ignited.

The day after the bushfires, I bought my little grey-eared dog and promptly named her Cinders. A photo of Cinders and Sparky adorns the wall, behind my piano.

Three years after Sparky died, I said goodbye to my beautiful, gentle, Cinders. She was sixteen years old. I asked God if I could have her for Christmas. He gave me my desire. She died three days after Christmas 2016 and now rests next to Sparky.

So much history has passed in my life. So many goodbyes and so many losses and hard times and yet that is only a fraction of the story.

Chapter 5 – What the Locusts Have Eaten
Puppies and Purple Tibouchinas

Looking back, I can see how God has walked beside me, bringing comfort, courage, restoration and yes even laughter in the midst of tears.

A Bunch of Nasturtiums

Early in 2014, I required surgery. What was to have been a simple keyhole operation became considerably more. God gave me a dream, which warned me of what was to happen, and gave me the peace I needed to get through it. Later I wrote of this experience. I share it with you now.

Standing on the edge of the deep, narrow gorge, I stared at the bridge, which stretched two thirds of the way across, and then – nothing, just empty space where the bridge should be. Trembling, I stepped closer to the bridge, my mind struggling to comprehend my predicament. Looking over the edge, it was a long way to the bottom. Casting my eyes up the other side, it looked as though truckloads of huge boulders had been tipped over the edge.

There was no other way. Climbing down was hard enough, but the ascent up seemed impossible. Scrambling over one boulder, searching for hand and footholds tearing skin off both my arms and legs, I was met by another boulder, and another, and still more large jagged rocks, until, exhausted I pulled my weary and bloodied body over the edge and stood once more on the ground.

Sensing I was not alone, I raised my head. Standing in front of me were three men. I knew they would not harm me. One of them stepped forward and handed me a bouquet of nasturtiums. 'Nasturtiums?'

Opening my eyes, still half asleep, I fumbled for the light switch of my bed lamp. Lying there and thinking of the dream, I know it is important.

'What are you saying God?

Sitting up and pushing my pillows behind me, I reach for my journal and pen. I must not lose the dream. I write it out while it's still graphic and real to me.

Though the Storms Rage
Yet Will I Dance

Thursday morning, two days from now, I am booked into hospital to have keyhole surgery to remove my gallbladder and with it, a golf ball sized gallstone.

'There is the possibility that you may have to undergo open surgery, but the most likely scenario is hospital and keyhole surgery on Thursday, home again on Friday.' The surgeon seemed quite confident in his prediction.

With that information, I inform my piano students of the week ahead, and tell my Saturday students to turn up for lessons.

This dream however is causing me to rethink. I know that the incomplete bridge is telling me that the easy way – e.g. keyhole surgery is not to be. The surgery is going to be an uphill, rocky road. I also know that the three men represent my Heavenly Father, Jesus and the Holy Spirit. 'But what do the nasturtiums represent?'

Getting out of bed, I collect my laptop from the study climb back into bed and google 'nasturtiums'.

'With the nasturtium, you get a flower that indicates that there will be a victory through a battle and conquest. Hundreds of years ago, army generals, when coming out of a battle, victorious, were given bunches of nasturtiums.'

I cancel all my lessons for the week.

Thursday morning, I find myself in theatre. The next thing I know, I am in the ward, hooked up to eight different things ... Saline drip, monitors, drains etc. My blood pressure is low. Thursday night, my blood pressure continues to drop until it is in the danger zone and a doctor is brought in to me in the middle of the night. People are busy all around me. I know I am not in a good place.

'It is OK, Lord, you have promised me a bunch of nasturtiums.'

Chapter 5 – What the Locusts Have Eaten
A Bunch of Nasturtiums

Friday night brings more drama as the hospital staff again keep a vigil, fearing a lung is about to collapse. As they busy themselves with caring for me. I lie there on my hospital bed. I am in complete peace. 'I know I'm going to come through this Lord. I'm waiting for my bunch of nasturtiums.'

Sometimes when it is impossible to dance physically, God enables one to dance in the Spirit, in His assurance, and His love.

This is one of those times.

Six days later I am allowed home. God had forewarned me in a dream, and given me the assurance that all would be well. 'Thank you, Father, for the victory, and for your peace. Thank you for my bunch of nasturtiums.

A String of Paradoxes

The definition of a paradox is 'a statement, doctrine or expression seemingly absurd or contradictory to the received belief or to what would naturally be believed but perhaps really true'.[VI]

This chapter has been a string of paradoxes, each paradox, a pearl in the precious necklace of my life.

In the section, 'Gaining Through Losing' I spoke of my loss. We were all severely pruned through Kola's illness and death, and yet looking back I can see in all of my sons and myself, abundant growth, compassion and strength, which developed through this period of loss.

'February 13' speaks of very precious mother/daughter moments given to me. Although my own daughter had died at the age of two, I experienced all of the major milestones in the life of a daughter through my involvement with friends, students and daughters-in-law. What an amazing paradox these years have been.

In 'Are You Willing?' God asks me a hard question. 'Are you willing to go wherever I send you and to do whatever I ask of you?' at a time when my pain was out of control and I could not put one foot in front of the other. A paradox? Surely so!

The 'Door of Hope Garden' grew out of ashes, pain and destruction, yet became beautifully restored.

In 'Amazing Grace' I spoke of being constantly told, 'You are only fit for the rubbish tip' and yet through the grace of God, I have accomplished much.

When Luke and I buried my little dog Sparky, it should have been so terribly sad and tear-filled, yet God organised the weather so that it became a Tragic Comedy, another paradox – tragedy and comedy combined.

Finally, in 'A Bunch of Nasturtiums', I experienced the paradox of total peace in the midst of the pandemonium around me in the hospital when people worked to save my life. In spite of the apparent evidence to the contrary, I knew I would come out of the situation victoriously.

How did I dance in a paradox? I followed my partner's steps. My partner was and is my God. Sometimes I danced through a situation hesitantly, sometimes in awe, sometimes in peace, sometimes in laughter, but always incredulous at the journey and its outcome.

Chapter 5 What the Locusts Have Eaten ~ For Reflection

1. As you think about what you have lost, can you also recall those things which have been restored to you?

Maybe, you are thinking, 'I have lost this, and nothing has been restored.'

It took three years for the loss from our house fire to be restored, but when it was, it was restored three-hundredfold. When my daughter died, the hope of mother-daughter experiences died with her. Decades later, God restored to me all those significant mother-daughter moments, through a chain of events and other young girls who embraced me as a mum.

2. Reflect on these verses and take heart:

Psalm 30:5 – *Weeping may remain for a night, (a season) but rejoicing comes in the morning.*

Isaiah 61: 3 – *[God will] provide for those who grieve in Zion, to bestow on them a crown of beauty instead of ashes, the oil of gladness instead of mourning and a garment of praise instead of a spirit of despair.*

Joel 2:25 – *I will repay you for the years the locusts have eaten*

Psalm 27: 13,14 – *I am still confident of this: I will see the goodness of the Lord in the land of the living. Wait for the Lord: be strong and take heart and wait for the Lord.*

Chapter 6 – Forgiveness, Faith and a Future

1. Forewarning
2. False Accusations
3. Getting Through It
4. Two Trees
5. Two Wolves

Forewarning

One morning, I woke early from a recurring dream. Three times in the dream, I was entering an extremely difficult situation. What the situation entailed, was hidden from me, but each time Jesus stood beside me. Slightly built and with dark brown, softly wavy hair, he looked at me with his deep, compassionate eyes. I knew he could see all of me, nothing hidden. I felt rather than heard him saying, 'I am here with you through the tough times. I am always with you. I will never leave you and I love and care for you very deeply.'

One month later, I was in the midst of a horrible situation culminating in me being accused of a crime I did not commit.

False Accusations

During this time, two friends were also facing false accusations, different people, different circumstances and different accusations. Have you ever been in a situation where you have been accused wrongly of words or actions, but found it seemingly impossible for the truth to be revealed? It devastates you. It devastated my friends and it devastated me.

Getting Through It

Two days after the terrible time when it happened to me, while still asleep, God impressed two bible verses on my mind. I got up, turned on my light and looked up those verses. They are:

Psalm 55:22 – *Cast your cares on the Lord and He will sustain you, he will never let the righteous fall.*

1 Peter 5:7 – *Cast all your anxiety on Him because he cares for you.*

Both texts began with 'Cast.' Casting is an action. Now was the time to exercise active faith – alive, believing and trusting.

I remembered Jesus standing beside me. I remembered his face and his beautiful, all seeing, compassionate eyes and I remembered what He told me. 'I am here with you through the tough times, I am always with you.'

Even when I stuff up, God still loves me, just as he did Abraham who lied, Jacob who cheated, Moses who murdered a man and Peter who denied Christ three times. All of them stuffed up, but God loved them, forgave them, trained them and used them mightily.

I knew what I had to do next. I had to forgive the person who had wronged me, and I needed to forgive myself and not allow bitterness to take root.

Two days after the accusation had been made, I woke early in the morning, about 2.am, switched on my bedside light and reached for my bible. Five texts were highlighted for me. I got my journal and pen and recorded them.

Hebrews 13:6 – *The Lord is my helper; I will not be afraid. What can man do to me?*

Though the Storms Rage
Yet Will I Dance

James 1: 2-4 – *Consider it pure joy my brothers, whenever you face trials of many kinds, because you know that the testing of your faith develops perseverance. Perseverance must finish its work so that you may be mature and complete, not lacking anything.*

James1:12 – *Blessed is the man who perseveres under trial, because when he has stood the test, he will receive the crown of life that God has promised to those who love Him.*

Matthew19:26 – *With man this is impossible, but with God all things are possible.*

Mark 9:23, 24 – *Everything is possible for him who believes. I do believe, help me overcome my unbelief.*

With God as my helper I will not be afraid or anxious and I will be joyful and persevere through this trial. For me alone it is impossible, but with God, all things are possible.

Jonathon, one of my sons, reminded me of something our American friend had told us to do when the going was tough during Kola's illness, and after his death. He told us to write down ten things each day to thank Jesus for. Jonathon has done this many times.

I began writing my daily list. I will share two of them with you. I found them such a positive, helpful thing to do.

10 Things I Thank God For

1. Cinders surviving the anaesthetic and coming home.
2. My friends, Lorrell, Rhonda, Mary-Lou, Eileen, Daryl, Jo.
3. The love and support of my children and my niece and nephews.
4. My garden.
5. My home.

Chapter 6 – Forgiveness, Faith and a Future
Getting Through It

6. That God cares for me and won't let me fall.

7. For Jesus letting me see His wonderful face, his eyes, his love.

8. For my car and that you kept me safe today despite my driving lapses and forgetting where I parked.

9. For kind people at the vets, the bank and the café.

10. For Jenny, Cassie and Des, my neighbours.

10 Things I Thank God For

1. Cinders is pain free and that she took the pain medication.
2. Lorrell coming again today, and inviting me for dinner again, even though I didn't go.
3. The tea drink which helps to calm my nerves.
4. 'The People's Friend' I got today.
5. Most of my garden flourishing. e.g. the Blue Ginger, the Garlic Vine with its mauve flowers and the trailing blue flowers in the basket – all in full bloom.
6. The sound of bees high up in the palm tree.
7. Being able to make the resolve and begin to eat for my health.
8. My iPhone, so I can ring family and friends.
9. My washing machine and Napisan, so that I could do Lorrell's wash (her machine has died), and my washing.
10. My brain was not as foggy today. I was calmer.

    I found herbal sleeping tablets and herbal tea which I made with milk and honey. Both these remedies helped me to have good, restful sleeps of a night.

Though the Storms Rage
Yet Will I Dance

I also booked sessions with a Christian psychologist. I had never been to a psychologist, but on the recommendation of a friend, I took this step.

Louise was compassionate, patient and knowledgeable. I only went five times but the help I received was invaluable. Firstly, I felt it was shameful to have to go, but I soon learnt how false this belief was. Secondly, she helped me with practical exercises, which helped to calm me.

She gave me breathing exercises to slow my breathing and muscle tightening and relaxing exercises to release tension. They really worked and were a large part of my being able to walk through this extremely stressful period of my life.

Louise gave me an exercise called 'Leaves in the River'. I was to imagine myself sitting beside a stream watching autumn leaves float by. As the leaves passed by, I was to throw or place my thoughts, fears, anger, sorrow, whatever I was feeling, into the leaves and allow those little leaf boats to carry those thoughts or feelings away. I could not imagine this, but Jesus had told me to cast my cares and anxiety onto him, so I imagined myself, sitting by the Sea of Galilee, looking out and seeing Jesus standing in a boat, just offshore.

This I could do, and what God told me to do and what my psychologist told me to do, came together.

The greatest help Louise gave me, was an understanding of where we were both coming from and why it caused such huge conflict.

The next day, God gave me a dream, which had several scenes. All of them showed me trying to do something and failing. Each time, what I had failed to do was done for me. I knew God was telling me to step back and do nothing. He is working it all out. The message was so clear. Let go and let God.

Sometime later, a visiting speaker to our church spoke to me.

Chapter 6 – Forgiveness, Faith and a Future
Getting Through It

'There has been an accusation against you. It is false. Brush it off. There will be reconciliation and when it happens you will be surprised. In the meantime, you are not to do anything. Let go and let God.'

After what had happened on that terrible day, even though I knew I was not guilty, I felt an absolute failure. I kept going to church because my pastors and my friends encouraged me to. Even so, I would sit alone and not talk to anyone, for I felt that I was a hypocrite. What right did I have to be there where people looked up to me and sought me out for help, when I had this terrible thing hanging over me?

Five weeks later, all that changed. A prophetic speaker, Isabelle Allum, came to our church. She gave prophetic words to most people there. This is the message she gave me.

'I heard God say, 'you are a safe place for many'. He is going to increase that safety and he is going to increase you more and more as a place of refuge for wherever you go people will know that refuge has arrived. There are great refuges around, but I heard the Lord saying, 'You are a safe place for many, and I am going to increase that safety.'

I stood at the front of the church and sobbed and sobbed as God poured His healing oil into all the recesses of my being. This was the opposite end of the spectrum to what I had experienced. I had been falsely accused and felt I had failed, but God's truth was that I had a future in Him. I stepped out of the last remnants of the effects of the false accusation and into the light, peace and victory of the truth of God.

Two Trees

That same day, Isabelle spoke of the two trees in the Garden of Eden.

One tree was the Tree of Knowledge of Good and Evil. The other tree was the Tree of Life. We choose to sit under one or the other of those two trees.

If we sit under the tree of Knowledge of Good and Evil, we live our lives with judgement, condemnation, criticism and everything that brings discouragement and death.

If we sit under the Tree of Life, we live our lives with mercy, forgiveness and everything that brings life.

We choose which tree we are under by the words we speak out. I knew I had to choose to speak only life, mercy and forgiveness to those around me. I had forgiven, now I had to speak only positives into and over this person's life. I got a sheet of paper and wrote down everything positive about that person who had wronged me.

Two Wolves

There is a Native American, Cherokee legend about two wolves. A young man was angry because a friend had done him an injustice. His old grandfather told him the following story:

'I too, at times, have felt a great hate for those who have taken so much, with no sorrow for what they do. But hate wears you down, and does not hurt your enemy. It is like taking poison and wishing your enemy would die. I have struggled with these feelings many times.' He continued, 'It is as if there are two wolves inside me. One is good and does no harm.

He lives in harmony with all around him, and does not take offense when no offense was intended. He will only fight when it is right to do so and in the right way.

But the other wolf, ah! He is full of anger. The littlest thing will set him into a fit of temper. He fights everyone, all the time, for no reason. He cannot think because his anger and hate are so great. It is helpless anger, for his anger will change nothing.

Sometimes, it is hard to live with these two wolves inside me, for both of them try to dominate my spirit.'

The boy looked intently into his Grandfather's eyes and asked, 'Which one wins, Grandfather?'

The Grandfather smiled and quietly said, "The one I feed."[VII]

Chapter 6 Forgiveness, Faith and a Future ~ For Reflection

1. Are you (or have you been) in a place where you have been falsely accused?

2. Because of this incident, are you carrying guilt, worthlessness, shame, anger, bitterness, grief or some other negative, soul-destroying emotion?

3. Have you spoken to God about it? What is he saying to you?

4. Have you sought professional help? I went to a Christian psychologist and her input into my life has been and is of immense value to me.

5. Are you still in close contact with your friends or your church and not allowing yourself to withdraw and become isolated?

6. Read the life stories of Moses, David, Peter and Jacob. They all fell very short of the ideal, yet each rose to do great things for God and their fellow men.

7. Which tree are you sitting under – the Tree of Knowledge or the Tree of Life?

8. Which wolf are you feeding?

Chapter 7 – Dancing Solo

1. Stage Fright
2. One Step at a Time
3. Helpers Along the Journey
4. Positives and negatives of Dancing Solo
5. Sick and Alone Overseas

Stage Fright

When I turned sixty, I gave myself the gift of a trip to the United Kingdom. I visited Leeds, my mother's birthplace, and spent five days in Cornwall, my paternal ancestors' homeland.

However, I'd also hoped to visit Austria and Germany one day, the birthplaces of Mozart, Beethoven, Haydn and other composers whose music I learnt to love, as I studied music and became a music teacher.

Of course, I wanted to visit Switzerland, home of Heidi, the main character of a book I loved as a child; and I dreamt of France, birthplace of Impressionism with the art of Monet and the music of Debussy.

I finally fulfilled this dream in 2015 at the age of sixty-eight, visiting fourteen countries in total.

One Saturday, just before I was to set off on my holiday, I totalled what I had saved to use on this trip for optional excursions, train fares and food. I was $300 short of what I had planned on taking. In the morning, I had told my friend, Mary Lou, 'Oh well, I'll just have to tighten my belt and eat less'.

'It's not finished yet,' Mary-Lou replied.

That night, my son Tim and his wife Rachel knocked on my door.

'Mum we have just been blessed and we want to bless you.' They handed over a wad of money.

'This is a gift, not a loan. We weren't allowed to say no, and neither are you!'

I began counting out the money. I got to three hundred dollars.

Though the Storms Rage
Yet Will I Dance

'This is all I'm short of,' I tried to hand the remainder of the money back.

'No, Mum, you must take it all.' Tears welled in my eyes, as I continued to count. They had given me $1000.

My concern over lack of funds was more than met. I had a healthy safety net for the five-and-a-half-week trip. Monday morning, I organised a cash card for my holiday. When I was handed the card, tears again threatened to overflow.

Although I had booked and paid for my trip eight months previously, it had been a financial struggle, with one thing after another. I had major surgery. This was followed by the removal of cataracts from both eyes, then an abscess from the surgery of the previous year. The sewer pipes needed replacing - $6000, the car needed work - $2000, a new room was made downstairs for my family $3000 - I had managed to pay for everything, but had gone to the wire every month.

While I kept working towards this trip, it seemed as though it was something nebulous, something in the distant future.

When I banked the money on Monday, I at last felt that the holiday was really going to happen – just one week before I was to board the plane.

This whole journey – the three years, and especially the previous twelve months – I likened to the journey made towards preparing for a recital or music exam. The practice, frustration, tears, tiredness and self-doubt belonged to both journeys.

....

I looked at my flight itinerary. I saw that I would be flying on a domestic flight from Brisbane to Melbourne and then an international flight from Melbourne to Dubai. There was just a little over an hour to transfer and book in myself and my luggage. How could I do that in such a short space of time available to me? Well, the first thing I did was – PANIC!

Chapter 7 – Dancing Solo
Stage Fright

I then decided that was useless, so at 1.45 am when I should have been asleep, I rang the airport and inquired, 'How do I accomplish this?'

Again, I thought of the process of giving a recital. First came the hours and months of preparation. Then came the night of the recital. I stood in the wings, as stage fright threatened to undo me. I breathed deeply, calmed myself and walked onto the stage.

The airport employee, on the other end of the phone spoke.

'We will book both flights, give you the boarding passes for both flights and book your luggage through direct to Dubai. There will be a transfer bus waiting for you, to take you to your aircraft at the International Terminal.'

I took a deep breath, relaxed and thanked the young lady who had given me this information.

Stage fright was over. I relaxed and was ready to go.

Ready for the performance.

Ready for my big adventure to Europe.

Ready for 'dancing solo'.

One Step at a Time

My bags were in the car, and Tim was in the driver's seat ready to take me to the airport. I opened the passenger door, and looked across at Tim.

'Okay! Let's do this!'

It was a positive comment, but in actual fact, I was apprehensive. I had planned, saved and worked towards this for years, and when the moment arrived, I was fearful of stepping out. Five weeks, fourteen countries, travelling alone.

'Mum, you'll be fine. It's time to begin 'dancing solo'.

I looked across at him,

'Yes, you're right, this is the chapter I'm writing, this is the walk I must walk, and I will do it – one step at a time. I had learnt that lesson several years previously, when I was diagnosed with Adrenal Exhaustion, a condition where the endocrine system simply closes down, no longer providing the body with the necessary elements to sustain it. Consequently, I found myself struggling to keep going. I was totally exhausted. I was advised to give up work, but because my music studio was my own business, I could not give up teaching. If I wanted to keep my students, then I had to keep going. I taught each lesson, and between each teaching session I slept.

At this time, I heard the song *One Day at a Time Sweet Jesus*. The words of that song and especially the chorus became my daily, and often my hourly prayer:

Though the Storms Rage
Yet Will I Dance

One day at a time sweet Jesus

That's all I'm asking from you

Just give me the strength to do every day

What I have to do.

Yesterday's gone sweet Jesus

And tomorrow may never be mine

Lord help me today, show me the way

One day at a time. [VIII]

This again became my prayer as I was about to set off on my journey. It was an adventure, and it was exciting, but anything new, especially when you are alone can be quite daunting! I resolved I would do it, one step at a time.

Helpers Along the Journey

Two days before the trip began, Pastor Charles prayed that God would put people beside me who would help me on my journey. I would see answers to this prayer over and over during the next five weeks.

On boarding the first plane in Brisbane, I entered the cabin and was told I had an aisle seat. When I got to my seat, I found I had all three seats, including a window seat to myself. I moved over to the window seat, and when we had ascended, I put the seat back, and stretched out. It was only a two-and-a-half-hour flight, but I was comfortable and was able to nod off for part of the trip.

I arrived in Melbourne at 10.30 pm. As I disembarked, an off-duty airline hostess, travelling with her husband and two sons, adopted me and guided me to the International check-in. There was no stress. I had my own personal guide!

Next, I went to the check-in. The person who served me asked to see my ticket. I asked for a window seat, but would take what I was given. You have to pay extra for a window seat. He looked at my ticket.

'You have a window seat, but there is someone next to you. Let me see if I can get you something better.'

'Yes! Look, I'll move you further forward, give you a window seat, and you now have three seats. You can spread out more and be comfortable.'

I was amazed, but he wasn't finished yet.

'Here, because the flight is delayed, I'll give you a $30 voucher. Take it and buy food and drink for yourself, but you must spend it in one shop.'

Though the Storms Rage
Yet Will I Dance

Thanking him, I moved on. The blessings were pouring down on me.

My next flight wasn't until 2.15 am – a three-and-a-half-hour wait. The voucher was dated for the 8th I was not flying out until early the morning of the 9th. The manager gave me an apple and elderberry drink, and gave me the receipt for an order, which I could get at 1.00 am. I found a quiet table, sat and began journaling. It was then nearly midnight. With the gift of the food voucher staggered over the next couple of hours, I would be able to stay awake till I needed to board my flight for Dubai. Once on the plane, with the seating arrangement given me, I'd be able to sleep.

It had been a good beginning to my Solo Dance. I'd left home six hours earlier and had flown the first leg of my journey. Already four different people had come alongside me and blessed me.

Thinking about it, this is a microcosm of my life; dancing solo, yes, but never alone.

Five days into my tour of Europe, I woke from a dream, very early in the morning, in my room at Barcelona, Spain.

In the dream, I was like Pilgrim (from *Pilgrim's Progress* by John Bunyan) walking my journey. As I came to each new section of my journey, I would be sent a 'helper'. Like an angel, she would sometimes recall an old song, sometimes sing a new song – but each time it would be the direction I needed to take, which enabled me to do that next section of my life. I had to state what it was that I needed. Sometimes it would be something lost that had to be regained; at other times, it would be something new. Then I would be sent helpers to co-journey that section, to sing the song and dance the dance till I knew it, and had travelled that section. At each new section, my guide would reappear, and I'd learn the next song or the next steps and helpers or companions would join me on that section of my journey.

Chapter 7 – Dancing Solo
Helpers Along the Journey

While on tour, I could see the practical application of my dream being played out as we travelled through various countries and many cities and locations on our way.

We had a wonderful tour director, John, who would prepare us for the next stop and the next, throughout our twenty-four days. He would give us information about the next city or highlight of the tour. This could be historical or geographical information. Often times it would be practical help. As we approached a new country, he would teach us key phrases in the new language – French, then Spanish, then Italian and onwards as we progressed from country to country.

As well as our tour director, we had many local guides. The local guide would be someone from a specific area who would be well versed in the culture, history, geography and specific information relevant to their own little patch of earth.

At Barcelona, we got out of our bus and walked to the Church of the Sacred Familia. This large and amazing church was designed by Gaudi and is still in the process of completion years after it was begun.

It is a huge tourist attraction, drawing thousands of visitors to see it. Consequently, the area is very congested. We were told to guard our belongings very carefully and were warned of especially dangerous locations, sections where we were crowded in on all sides by many people. This is where pickpockets would mingle and steal from the unwary.

Our local guide led us, and our tour guide walked behind, watching over us and protecting us. It reminded me of the story of the Israelites when they were in the wilderness with Moses and they had a pillar of cloud by day and a pillar of fire by night. Sometimes the pillar of cloud went ahead and sometimes it would be behind them, guarding them.

In my own personal life, I knew that I also had both a foreguard and a rearguard watching over me.

Positives and Negatives of Dancing Solo

It was day 15 of my European Tour. We began the day by boarding a boat and going to the Murano Glass Blowing factory and display centre. Murano is a small island in the large saltwater lagoon just off Venice. Several people bought things. I did not. While the glassware was stunning, it was also very expensive and not anything that I needed.

Next, we caught another boat back to Old Venice where we were to go on a guided tour.

We disembarked and made our way as a group to St Mark's Square. We walked along the promenade beside the water and soon turned right, into the square. Pigeons perched on the beautiful, old lamp posts. I turned away from my group and took a photo. When I turned back, my tour group were nowhere to be seen. Thankfully, I knew where we would be meeting three hours later, so I decided to make the most of my time alone.

After walking around St Mark's Square, I made my way down to where we'd be boarding our boat to Burano for our excursion that afternoon. I made a cup of tea (I had filled my thermos that morning) and had lunch of a Danish roll with Nutella (a chocolate and nut spread), four small sweet biscuits and grapes, which I had collected from the table at breakfast. I sat and caught up with my journal.

I still had another two hours to wait. St Mark's Square floods eighty times a year. This day was one of those times.

The square was filling up with water because of the high tide. They put out raised platforms to walk on but because of the hundreds of people milling around and trying to walk on the platforms, chances were that you would end up in the murky water, which was rapidly covering the Square. If you sat on a seat at any of the al fresco restaurants in St Mark's Square

Though the Storms Rage
Yet Will I Dance

without buying anything, even if all the seats were empty, you would be asked to get up and leave so I moved to the seating near the boat terminal.

That afternoon we boarded another boat and sailed to Burano, a beautiful small island. All of the houses, doors and shutters were painted in different bright colours and the windowsills were decorated with window boxes and pot plants. The steeple of the church leaned at an angle. I wandered up and down many lanes, a lot of them divided by canals. The boats were also painted in bright colours. Sitting on his chair, beside the canal, an old fisherman was making a fishing-net with a bone needle. I took his photo.

I was supposed to have connected with my group for lunch in one of the cafes on the island. I got so carried away, taking photos and exploring that I completely lost track of time and missed out on lunch.

It was a good day. A day I spent largely by choice on my own. I was at peace with myself, and the world. I liked dancing solo, free to think my own thoughts without noisy invasion, free to be myself.

One of the positives of dancing solo is 'open doors'. The willingness to step out on one's own opens doors to many new and exciting adventures – countries to be explored, new people to meet, new cultures to experience.

Whatever the perimeters of a life, the ability and willingness to expand those perimeters will enrich your life. It might be just getting to know a next-door neighbour, or it could take you around the world. It could be picking up a pencil and doing miniature sketches, or it could be painting a large canvas. It doesn't matter how big or small. What matters is that we allow and enable ourselves to step out and dance solo if that is what is needed to reach new, or as yet unfulfilled dreams and goals.

Chapter 7 – Dancing Solo
Positives and Negatives of Dancing Solo

Independence

Dancing solo, of course requires independence.

After my daughter's death, we moved to a college town, where my husband, Kola, completed his degree. My independence was severely challenged as pressure was put on us to move into 'married student' quarters so that I would have the 'peer' support that the 'powers that be' thought I required.

I knew that what my family and I needed was solitude and space where we could work out our grief in our own way and care for our two young sons and each other.

It required a huge dose of independence on my part (labelled stubbornness by some) to achieve what I knew was right for my family and myself.

While independence can be a positive when dancing solo, it can alternatively be a huge negative.

Independence can isolate you. If you carry independence to the place where you believe you don't need help or input from anyone else, then it can take you to a very lonely place.

Less independent or less confident people could see an independent person as a very real threat because it is so far removed from their own reality.

Independence can be seen as rejection. I have fallen into this trap many times, I am very sorry to say.

One instance occurred soon after my husband's death. I'd bought a new house and needed to thoroughly clean our rental house and pack all of our possessions for the move. My best friend, Lorna, immediately said she would be over to help me pack and clean. In my extreme independence, I refused all help choosing to do everything myself. I was quite capable of doing it myself. I liked doing it myself. The constant hard work was a therapy to me. But I totally overlooked the relational aspect of my best friend's offer. I hurt her badly. I never intended to hurt her, but I hurt her nonetheless.

My children have also been hurt by my unwillingness to accept help. It has been a very hard lesson for me to learn. I pray that now I can see things from a much wider viewpoint than just my own and not make this mistake again.

Communication

When dancing solo, communication breakdown can be an easy trap to fall into. I have lived alone now for eighteen years. I make my own decisions and act on them. That is fine, but I have so often left people so totally in the dark, because I have not communicated with people, causing confusion and instability within different relationships. For years, I would go to a party or a meeting and when I'd had enough, I would pick up my bag and exit without a word to anyone. My thinking would be, 'They won't even miss me!' But then I would get that 'follow-up' phone call. 'Are you okay? Why did you leave?'

Thankfully, I have now learnt to say goodbye and at least partially explain my actions. I might live alone, but I do not live in isolation. Because of that I need to be very careful that I communicate properly, so as not to confuse or hurt anybody.

Resilience

I almost gave up my dream of becoming a music teacher. I had progressed quickly through my grades, both piano and theory, gaining honours (85+%) for most of my exams. That came to an abrupt halt when

Chapter 7 – Dancing Solo
Positives and Negatives of Dancing Solo

I sat for my Grade Seven piano exam. I got stage fright. I had a total mental block and could not remember or perform anything. I failed. I was totally devastated. Crying bucketloads of tears, I told myself I was not good enough to be a music teacher.

A week of wallowing in self-pity convinced me this was not the place to be. I enrolled in the next examination session and redid my exam. This time, with my nerves under control, I played well, gaining good high marks once again. Eventually I realised that the failure could be turned to good use by encouraging other people to keep going, rather than allowing a failure to cripple them and rob them of their dreams.

At the time, I did not have a name for this experience. Now I do. It is called resilience.

I learnt that falling is part of learning to walk, and that failures along the way are part of learning.

Mahatma Gandhi wrote:

'Strength does not come from winning. Your struggles develop your strengths. When you go through hardships and decide not to surrender, that is strength.' [IX]

The definition of resilience I really relate to says:

'Resilience is very different than being numb. Resilience means you experience, you feel, you fail, you hurt, you fall, but you keep going.' [X]

Sometimes the pain of what we experience seems too much to bear, and yet to get through it we must face the pain and move through it.

There are times in our lives when it is okay to lean. A trusted friend, relative, counsellor or psychologist is essential to us at such times.

I remember a dream I had during a difficult time a few years back. I was at the entrance to a long, very dark tunnel. I knew I had to walk through that tunnel, but was afraid. As I took the first couple of steps, I felt a hand take mine and begin to walk with me. I knew the hand belonged to God. As I walked through that tunnel, holding God's hand, my fear left me. Not only that, but the darkness dissipated until I found myself walking in bright light. As I walked, God enveloped me with His presence and His joy, and I was strengthened to walk through this tough time. There is a text in the bible, which actually says that *'The joy of the Lord is my strength."* (Nehemiah 8:10).

There is a downside to resilience and strength - intolerance. Having learnt resilience, I need to recognise that others around me may be struggling and they need support and love, not impatience and intolerance.

I need to remember that I too have walked through some very hard times, so I now need to be willing to walk with my friend who has cancer, with my friend who has just become widowed, or is walking through their own dark tunnel of pain and despair, until they also learn resilience.

Confidence

A few years ago, a very dear friend of mine walked through betrayal, separation and divorce. It was not an easy walk, and especially at the outset it was very difficult. Financially, emotionally, whichever way you looked at it, the beginning of her journey was fraught with hurdles, which at the time seemed insurmountable. Her self-confidence was almost non-existent.

A deluge of forms threatened to drown her. Forms for separation, for settlement, for getting money to live on, forms from banks and other institutions where her ex-husband's name had to be removed, or her name became the sole name when it hadn't even been on the previous documents. Forms and more forms and then more forms!

Chapter 7 – Dancing Solo
Positives and Negatives of Dancing Solo

Previously her husband had controlled everything so that form-filling was not part of her experience. Filling in a form was a terrifying experience. Each new form brought her back to this place of feeling totally inadequate for the task.

Despite this, I watched an amazing transformation in her. Fear and trembling were replaced by hesitancy. Hesitancy was replaced by a small, experimental confidence. She was this beautiful, fragile, rosebud, opening its petals to the sunlight until eventually, she became a confident woman, a rose, fully open to experience her world. Forms no longer brought fear. She went back to study and graduated with a Diploma of Counselling and then a Spiritual Director's qualification.

I also went through a transformation, growing in confidence with each new experience after the death of Kola. I did not begin with the big European trip I've already mentioned. I began with baby steps. I travelled overseas for the first time when I was fifty-two, just six months after my husband died. I travelled from Brisbane, Australia, to Albany, New York State, in the United States. We flew into Los Angeles International Airport at night. As we landed, after fourteen hours in the air, I thought, 'I'm never going to get out of this airport!' It was really daunting. I needed to stay for a couple of hours somewhere in that airport, before boarding another plane to take me another seven hours across the continent to New York. As the plane prepared to land, we were given clear directions. All I had to do was follow them. Fourteen hours later, after being delayed in New York for five hours due to a blizzard, I finally arrived in Albany and met my friends who then looked after me for the next three weeks.

A year later I took myself to New Zealand for a week-long coach tour of the South Island.

A couple of years later I went on a three-week tour of the United Kingdom. At the end of that tour I travelled by public transport through England, found my own accommodation and spent the next five days exploring the coastal paths, through woodlands and to neighbouring villages.

Though the Storms Rage
Yet Will I Dance

In 2015, I travelled alone to Dubai for a couple of days and then on to a 24-day coach tour through twelve European countries. At the conclusion of that tour I then travelled by train to Cambridge, England before travelling to Japan.

The first trip, I was cared for by friends, then each succeeding trip, I travelled for longer time periods to more countries, becoming more confident and adventurous.

Gaining confidence is like learning to fly. Most birds take very short flights first, testing and strengthening their wings, each successive flight becoming longer, their wings becoming stronger. So it is with us. We take small steps first, and as our confidence grows, we stretch ourselves further.

All I had to do, and all my friend had to do was to take that first faltering step. All the other steps just followed.

As I stepped into my new world of singleness, I learnt many things. I needed to treat myself kindly, but I would not 'baby' myself. For me, setting goals helped me to always move forward. I have close friends who let me use them as a sounding board. Indeed, we are sounding boards to each other. I have learnt to laugh at myself.

Perhaps the hardest thing for me personally was to allow myself to have time-out, time just for me. I have learnt to like 'me' and to be confident in the person I have become.

Alone or Lonely

Looking back over my life, and particularly those years when I was 'dancing solo', eleven years before my marriage and now nineteen years of widowhood, I can honestly say that I have never been truly alone until recently when my little sixteen-year-old dog, Cinders died.

Chapter 7 – Dancing Solo
Positives and Negatives of Dancing Solo

The house was empty, but that extreme loneliness only lasted a couple of days. I have family, friends, neighbours, and yes, even strangers who have walked with me along my journey.

I remember one particular occasion in 2007 when travelling alone in England. I had just spent three wonderful days with my friend Kelli in Warrington, England. She had dropped me off at Liverpool Station where I had boarded the first of three trains to Looe.

While trying to find my way to the correct platform at Plymouth, a woman behind me verbally attacked me, throwing abuse at me for no apparent reason that I could see. I got into a lift to take me to the platform I needed. This woman got into the lift with me and continued her abuse in front of all the others in the lift. I turned to her, 'If I have hurt you in any way, I am sorry, but I am a stranger in your country trying to find my way'.

When the lift door opened, we all got out. This woman and her family made their way towards the canteen. A railway attendant turned to me and asked me where I was going. He then told me I was on the correct platform, but there was a waiting period before the train left and he directed me towards the canteen.

'No thank you, I have a thermos of hot chocolate and food with me.' Kelli had provided for my journey and no way did I want to rub shoulders with that woman again.

I sat on the platform seat and got out my thermos and sandwiches. By this time, I felt tears gather in my eyes and I was struggling to keep it together.

A tall, stately, well-dressed man came and sat beside me and began to talk to me. When it was time to board, he helped me on with my luggage and sat beside me. He became my travel guide and stayed with me until the station before I reached my destination. Before he left, he explained to me that the next train I was to board had its own line and platform adjacent to the one where I would leave this train. I often wonder, was he an angel sent to comfort me at that time? I just know that I was comforted, and the

Though the Storms Rage
Yet Will I Dance

tears disappeared. At a time when I felt totally alone, God sent this man (angel) to me so that for the remainder of my journey I was no longer alone.

Being 'alone' can wear many guises. As a child, I felt alone because I didn't have the emotional support from family, and was 'different' to my peers.

As a college student, I was alone, although I was one of hundreds. Some students had siblings or friends with them. Others were alone but still had financial or emotional backing from those at home. I had neither.

Sometimes being alone is by choice. Very often it is forced onto you. Widowed, divorced or single by choice, you are alone.

Indeed, many people are married but very much 'alone', even within that relationship or lack thereof.

So, what is the answer to this state of aloneness? For me, it has and is and always will be, that I have a God who watches over me, guiding me and sending me the right person in season.

Being alone and being lonely are two very different things. You can have one without the other. Being alone and dancing solo can be a very precious and exciting place to be.

Sick and Alone Overseas

It was 8.30 pm when I finally arrived at my Bed and Breakfast house in Cambridge. Earlier that afternoon, I had disembarked from my coach, collected my travel bag and waved farewell to all those who I had travelled with through twelve countries in Europe for the past twenty-four days. It had been a wonderful experience, a dream come true. Now, after two connecting train journeys, I was ready for bed. A cough, which had begun on the last days of the tour, was now wracking my body. I climbed into bed, just wanting to sleep, but the coughing had intensified to the point of dry retching. Sleep was impossible. The next morning, my hostess brought my breakfast to my room. The following night I saturated my bed with sweat from a fever. I couldn't eat, couldn't sleep, and couldn't stop coughing. My bedroom was all I saw of Cambridge.

Reversing my journey of three days earlier, I returned to London, and on to Heathrow Airport. Having emptied my bag of some things, it now weighed only 16kg, but it felt as though it was 160kg. Changing platforms, going up and down stairs while dragging my suitcase behind me – the journey was a nightmare. Still feverish and coughing relentlessly while having to travel, and changing trains three times, it seemed like an impossible task. I felt so totally alone and helpless. It felt as though I was on a conveyor belt that I could not get off.

Once at the airport, I managed to get through the process of boarding an international flight. I don't know how I accomplished it, but I did.

Sitting between two beautiful young Japanese people, I settled in for a long twelve-hour flight to Tokyo. The plane had no air vents that I could see. I was still very hot and feverish. The hostess had given us a warm cloth to wash our face and hands before eating. I did not eat but kept my cloth, and as the hours passed, I desperately needed to cool myself. I

Though the Storms Rage
Yet Will I Dance

had no paracetamol, which could have helped to get my temperature down. I had a watered-down bottle of orange juice, so I soaked and wet my face, neck and wrists with this diluted juice. If the young people noticed, they said nothing. I continued this regime throughout the trip. When we landed at Haneda Airport, Tokyo, twelve hours later, I was too weak to walk. After all the other passengers had left the plane, the cabin crew helped me to the door of the aircraft where two young women got me into a wheelchair. They then got me through customs, collected my luggage and put me into a taxi, which took me to my hotel. I don't know any of their names, but I thank them all for helping me.

A dignified, gentleman with greying hair, probably about my age, met me. On the way, he stopped to show me where I could get cold water and ice. Once in my room, he looked at me and commented,

'You are very tired'.

'Yes, I am and sick too.' He left, and I climbed into bed to cough my way through yet another night.

In the morning, I heard a soft knock on my door. I didn't get up, but called, 'Come in'. I didn't think about my door being locked. It didn't matter. A gentle, softly spoken woman entered.

'I am so worried about you. Can I get you anything? My office is next door to you, and I heard you coughing.'

'Oh yes, can you please get me some ice and cold water.'

Her name was Kie, and she was the Room Division Housekeeper Leader for the Shiba Park Hotel in Tokyo. For the next three days, Kie and her staff kept me supplied with ice, cold water, tea and clean towels. I remained in bed for those three days. Although I was booked on day-tours to see Tokyo and to travel to Mt Fujiyama and Hakane National Park, I went nowhere. But I was not alone anymore. Kie and her girls cared for me.

Chapter 7 – Dancing Solo
Sick and Alone Overseas

The day I was to leave, I left my room at midday and went down to the Foyer to check out, taking my luggage with me. I was going to sit in the lounge off the foyer for the next three hours. Kie, however had rung down to the front desk, told them I was sick and asked that they take me back to my room.

I returned to my room, sank onto the bed and slept. Three hours later I returned to the foyer. The hotel manager came over to me. He handed me a gift of two beautiful handkerchiefs illustrated with cherry blossoms, a dancing girl in a kimono, Mt. Fuji and Lake Ashi, along with an origami swan. He also handed me his card.

'Please, you must come back. We wait for you. Here is my card, please stay in touch with us.'

Kie came down from her office on the seventh floor. She also gave me her card and re-iterated what Masaomi, the manager, had just said,

'We wait for you, you must come back.' She also gave me a gift and others in the front office moved forward showering me with their gifts.

I was leaving for Australia from Narita Airport, which is 70 km out of Tokyo. A transfer bus does a circuit of picking up people from various hotels.

When the bus arrived, Kie, Masaomi and three other staff members all came with me, and lined the outside of the hotel to wave me goodbye.

I saw very little of Japan, only what I saw as the bus took me to the airport. However, I saw and experienced the hearts of some very gentle, special people.

Yes, I will return to Japan and to Shiba Park Hotel.

It is easy to dance solo when everything is easy; when there are no hurdles to jump and when you are well. This last week of my trip was very hard. I referred to it as being a nightmare, especially when I was travelling and dragging my luggage behind me up and down stairs and from platform

Though the Storms Rage
Yet Will I Dance

to platform. However, even during this very difficult time, I had beautiful people ready to help me at almost every stage of my journey. No matter the circumstances, it is my choice to dance or not.

Chapter 7 Dancing Solo ~ For Reflection

1. When you are 'dancing solo', the journey at times can be quite daunting. Have you ever looked at the journey of life ahead of you and wondered how you could even begin the journey, let alone complete it?

2. When life ahead seems more than you can handle, can you break it down into manageable segments? Like the song, can you ask Jesus, 'Lord help me today, show me the way, one day at a time'?

3. Can you recall people who have been there for you, along life's journey?

4. Are you alone? Are you lonely? Do you maybe know someone who is living alone and who may be lonely? What can you do, or who could you connect with to make life not so lonely?

5. If you are living solo, can you list the positives of your life?

6. What would you like to do, to expand the perimeters of your life? What new door would you like to open?

7. Are you independent? What are the positives of independence? What are the negatives? Where do you fit?

8. Communication can be a real problem when you are living alone. What are your communication skills like?

9. 'Resilience means you experience, you feel, you fail, you hurt, you fall but you keep going. How resilient are you? Can you help someone, who is struggling through a hard time, to keep going during a difficult time, and in so doing, build resilience?

Though the Storms Rage
Yet Will I Dance

10. In what situations are you tolerant or intolerant?

11. Do you struggle, trying to do new things, and to step out alone? Do you have something you would really like to do, but are afraid to do it? If you can, share your dream with someone who you can trust, break your dream down into manageable steps and then take that first faltering step. Be excited!!

Chapter 8 – Bridal Waltz

1. Chandelier of Orchids
2. Sydney Trip
3. Mourning into Dancing
4. Come Closer
5. A Single White Daisy

Chandelier of Orchids

I lay in bed and stared in awe at my ceiling. A chandelier hung from where my fan/light normally hung. But this was no ordinary chandelier.

Whether a dream or a vision, I don't know. It appeared and felt so totally real.

The chandelier was made of white orchids, interspersed with tiny, delicate yellow orchids. It reached from the ceiling, right down to me as I lay in bed. The exquisite and fragrant blooms were like a huge wedding bouquet. They surrounded me with their fragrance and beauty.

As I lay, surrounded by this chandelier of orchids, some of the flowers brushed against my arm, and the gentle touch of them awakened in me a sense of wonder, of belonging, and of total peace and knowing I was not alone. I don't know how long I lay there enveloped by this amazing symbol of love. It was not a fleeting moment but an enduring space in time.

As the chandelier faded away, I continued to lie there and ponder over what I had just experienced.

I knew that God had reached down to me and surrounded me with this most wonderful gift—a bridal bouquet, an expression of God's love for me.

Sydney Trip

Several years ago, when I was first widowed and feeling alone and vulnerable, God showed me in His word, and then through His protection, that I was His and He would care for me and my children.

Six months after Kola's death, was the first time that God highlighted for me that Jesus, my Lord and Saviour, was now my husband, and in that, He was my provider and my protector.

My journal entry of the 07-03-00 records how it all happened.

Our trip to Sydney had been planned for some time. A friend was coming over from the USA to take a series of meetings and I knew that my sons and I should be there. Then on the Wednesday, two days before we were to leave, I received the following email which had been sent to all those who would be attending those meetings.

'I believe that I have received a message from the Lord. We have family travelling down from Qld this Friday. In my spirit, I feel Satan may try and cause a car accident and even try to kill them. It is the Kilchester family. Some of you know them, some of you don't. Please pray against satanic attack for the Kilchester family and friends. Pray for their protection and a safe trip.'

When we first received it, it threw us, and then I remembered reading that these messages were usually warnings, sent to us, for us to pray or repent so that the impending calamity could be averted.

I tried not to think too much about it, as I had an interview for a teaching position, only two hours away; a position, which I subsequently received later that same day. However, I rang two friends, Ella and Jackie, who then prayed for our safety, along with several other people who Santo had petitioned via email. Santo was the pastor of the church where the meetings were to be held.

Though the Storms Rage
Yet Will I Dance

Thursday morning, 6.30 am, Luke's car wouldn't start, so I drove him to work. On the way Luke kept saying, 'I can smell gear oil'.

The car was booked in for a service to be completed by 1.00 pm. We didn't get the car till 6.00 pm. It was automatic transmission fluid, they told us, and No! They didn't fix the problem. They thought it was just a pipe that needed to be replaced. By now I had become agitated. I didn't know whether we should travel to Sydney to attend the meetings or not – a 1300 km trip one-way (2600 km return).

I had believed that I should go especially for my two sons who were travelling with me. Tim's grip on God was really tenuous, as he was struggling badly with grief over his father's death six months earlier. Now with car problems on top of the warning we'd received, I began to waver.

The boys sat on my bed and we tried to decide what we should do. After some discussion, I told the boys to go to bed, and I would wait to see what God would say during the night hours, then we would make our decision.

Sometime later in the night, I awoke with the words of a hymn repeating over and over in my mind:

'The gates of hell cannot prevail against the army of the Lord.'

I turned my light on and picked up my bible. I knew God was talking to me. I asked myself, 'Is there a text in the bible that the hymn was based on?'

I looked up the concordance in the back of my bible and found Matthew 16:18 – '... *on this rock I will build my church, and the gates of Hades will not overcome it'*

I then noticed a cross-reference to Isaiah 54:17. Turning to Isaiah, I felt impelled to read the whole chapter. Although it referred specifically to the Israelites, God was using that chapter to speak to me. During the night, God spoke to me through his word, dealing with not one issue, but four issues of great relevance to me at this time.

Chapter 8 – Bridal Waltz
Chandelier of Orchids

Verses 4,5. *Remember no more the reproach of your widowhood. For your Master is your husband – The Lord Almighty is his name –*

I had been widowed six months.

Verse. 11. – *O afflicted city, lashed by storms and not comforted.*

My family had taken a very severe lashing from the storms of life, and while I had been very much comforted by the presence of God in my life, my oldest son was having an immense struggle.

V.13. *All your sons will be taught by the Lord and great will be your children's peace.*

This was my prime reason for this trip – that my sons, my oldest especially, would find his way back to God, and that all my sons would be taught by God and know His peace.

Verse.15 – *Whoever attacks you will surrender to you.*

Verse. 17 - *No weapon forged against you will prevail.*

We had been given a warning of Satan's attack on us, and here was God's answer. We would be safe. At 5.00 am next morning, I woke the boys and we set out on our trip. The trip was not without event, yet no harm came to any of us.

The most significant thing that happened to us on the way down to Sydney was that the entire underside of our car was coated with a liberal spraying of molasses, from a very sticky trail covering 100 km. A truck carrying the molasses, obviously had sprung a leak, and it deposited its load over the 100km distance. At Kempsey, we pulled up at traffic lights and the road was thick with it.

A State Emergency Service utility backed up behind us and stopped all traffic, one car behind us. As the wheels drove in the molasses, the sticky stuff was picked up and effectively sprayed over the entire car. At first, we thought this was funny, but looking back, I believe it was part of God's plan to keep us safe.

On the return trip, heavy rain washed it all off again, and the day we arrived back home, in the afternoon the car broke down, a pipe split, leaking quantities of transmission fluid. Water was also escaping from somewhere. I'd made a ten-minute trip late that night, and had to be towed home.

Did God provide his own glue for the trip and then washed it all off again when it was no longer needed?

It was not only during the trip to and from Sydney that we saw God's hand of protection over us.

On Saturday night, we were returning to a friend's home in the mountains around midnight. I was travelling in a car with Karen, the lady who was billeting us. The boys were following behind. The winding road up to Karen's home was very steep and narrow.

We heard the screeching of brakes, and looked back to see that the boys had spun out on a bend, stopping short of a tree. The accelerator had jammed, the car had accelerated and as Jonathon hit the brakes, the car spun. That was the only bend in the mountains where the boys would have had any clearance. Again, we were all safe, shaken but safe, and thankful to God for protection.

Sunday afternoon we were given a treat. Jonathon was keen to see and to cross the Sydney Harbour Bridge. We crossed over the bridge without any hassles, but Jonathon didn't really see much because he was driving. Not long after coming over we took a wrong turn, which took us in a large circle re-crossing the harbour on another bridge and providing us with views of the bridge from several different angles. Tim and Jonathon exchanged seats, and we re-crossed the bridge, this time with Jonathon in the passenger seat. I am convinced that God delights in giving His children treats.

Chapter 8 – Bridal Waltz
Chandelier of Orchids

On the return trip home, we encountered a large storm, which spanned hundreds of kilometres. The rain was heavy, creating a lot of water on the road. As we drove, a small utility passed us, driving too fast, and I commented on it. He then passed the car in front, giving no distance between them, and sending spray into the air, higher than the cars. Oncoming traffic was approaching from the other direction, but he somehow managed to pass without disaster.

A short while later we had to pull off the road to allow an ambulance to pass. A small utility had taken out another car, and gone off the road. It was the same utility. I exhaled deeply as I witnessed that accident. I knew that what I had just seen was meant for us, but that God had intervened and had protected us. I was shaken but at the same time so thankful to God.

Just after passing the accident we saw the most incredible rainbow any of us has ever seen. At one point, it spanned the road and went ahead of us. The colours were vivid and after completing the spectrum it almost repeated it without a break. A second rainbow shone out a little way off from the main one.

We were having trouble with the demister, so we pulled into a garage in Tamworth, where the boys were able to fix it. The heavy rain and the wind cleared as they repaired the demister, and we were able to continue our journey under a starlit sky. However, we had forgotten to fill the petrol tank, and further down the road the petrol light was on. I'd estimated we still had 15 km to go before reaching Uralla, the next town.

'We're not going to make it Mum,' Tim held the steering wheel steady, while glancing at me.

Jonathon spoke up.

'Why not ask God to help us? After all He has been with us all along.' We agreed.

Though the Storms Rage
Yet Will I Dance

The car finally ran out of petrol with the town still ahead of us, but I recognised a line of poplars along the right of the highway. I knew this road. I grew up in Tamworth and had relatives in Armidale. I had travelled this road many times.

'Tim, put the car into neutral, it's downhill, only slightly, but downhill none the less, all the way into town.'

We rolled four kilometres into town, past the first service station, which was closed, into the second station and right up to the petrol pump.

We arrived home, at 2.30 am Monday morning. There had been plenty of opportunities for disasters and yet God had been faithful and brought us safely home.

Mourning into Dancing

Not long after Kola passed away, I began going to church again. A very popular song at the time was *I Shall Turn Your Mourning into Dancing*. Each week I would walk into the school auditorium where church was held. I would join in the worship and be happy to be there. At some point in the service, however, they would invariably sing that song and I would have to leave the building and walk around the school grounds until I had pulled myself together. When I had stopped crying, I would get in my car and drive home. From previous experience with the loss of a loved one, I knew that my grief would abate with time. But right then the wound was too raw, the grief too deep.

Eighteen months after Kola's death I travelled to Albany, New York to visit my friends who were in ministry. While I was there, we travelled to various cities and towns and I joined in the ministry with them.

While ministering at Allentown, Pennsylvania, a woman who was visiting from the Toronto Airport Church approached me and prophesied over me.

'God is giving you a garden, a spiritual garden to walk through and from which you will gain peace, strength and encouragement.' The next day, we visited a beautiful woman called Eleanor. She had been at death's door. My friend had been told by God she was going to get better, and we prayed healing over her.

She sat in a chair in the corner of the lounge room with a rug over her legs.

'I miss playing the piano,' she said. She was legally blind and unable to sit at her piano. Her husband wasn't a pianist, so I played for about fifteen minutes. I played old hymns, such as *What a Friend*, *The Old Rugged*

Though the Storms Rage
Yet Will I Dance

Cross and *Whispering Hope*. Eleanor asked for *Back of the Clouds.* She had the music, so although I didn't know it, I was able to play it for her.

When we left, she was standing at the door, waving goodbye. My friends told me that Eleanor had cried while I played *The Old Rugged Cross.* Weeks later, after returning home to Australia, I heard that this dear lady had indeed been healed.

While driving home to Albany the next day, I had a very special experience. I sat in the back seat with Joyce who was part of the team, while Eoin and Joyce's husband sat in the front. Eion put on a CD of piano music. They were old hymns like the ones I'd played for Eleanor. I wanted to go deep into that music, so I closed my eyes and let it take me.

I found myself seeing a passing panorama. God took me on His own sightseeing tour of his High Country. Very high, steep mountains, with waterfalls and stone bridges, high meadows of rich green grass and bright yellow flowers.

He took me into the clefts of rocks, along rock walls and past more waterfalls, high up to the snow-covered crags and the billowing clouds, which deepened from pink to red. This was God's Garden in the High Country. I love God's High Country.

Back in Albany that night, I attended a combined-churches meeting at Our Saviour's Lutheran Church. During worship, we sang *I Will Turn Your Mourning into Dancing*. This time, I felt joy, I prayed for more joy, closed my eyes, listened to the music and the words of the song and let it soak into me. I twirled around on the spot, and I knew that God was indeed, turning my mourning into dancing.

Two days later, Ella and I travelled from Albany to Buffalo, on the border of New York State and Canada. At one point during the trip, I closed my eyes and saw a picture of a fairground while Ella drove. A jester dressed in his colourful satin costume, turned to me and winked. I opened my eyes and turning to Ella commented, 'A jester just winked at me!' Shortly afterwards we pulled into a rest area that not only had petrol and

Chapter 8 – Bridal Waltz
Mourning into Dancing

gas, but also a selection of shops offering food, magazines and souvenirs. I selected some souvenirs for my family and moved to the checkout. While waiting to be served, I looked back to the shelves where I had selected some gifts. Standing there was a life-sized statue of a woodsman dressed in a check shirt and heavy boots. I was thinking, 'That wasn't there before'. I continued to stare until the 'statue' gave me a gappy smile. It was missing several teeth! I immediately felt rather stupid, thinking that he may have thought I was chatting him up.

I blurted out, 'I'm sorry, I thought you were a statue'. Even as I spoke, I was thinking, 'Yeah! That's going to help!', and burst into a fit of the giggles. I looked at Ella, and she wasn't doing any better than me.

'Quick, let's get out of here!' Somehow, I managed to pay for my purchases, and we hurried to our car. For many miles one or the other of us would burst out laughing, setting the other one off, until we both were laughing uncontrollably.

Well, my jester sure achieved his purpose. I had not laughed like that for years. God was busy turning my grief into joy, my tears into laughter and my mourning into dancing.

Come Closer

I never learned to dance when I was young because I belonged to a church that didn't approve of dancing. However, I took it up at age sixty-eight.

Now I had the opportunity. A friend asked me if I would go ballroom dancing with him. I jumped at the chance to dance.

'Yes, but I don't know how to dance. Would you be willing to teach me some dances at home before I get up on the dance floor?'

When we began, he demonstrated my steps and got me to repeat them after him until I knew them. Then he took my hands and led me in the dance. I did alright but knew I needed to dance better. After a couple of sessions, my friend looked at me.

'Today we are going to dance differently. We are going to get close.'

He took my hand and held me so that our bodies were touching. Then we turned on the music and danced. Now we were dancing as one. I could feel and anticipate his moves – to the right, the left, forward and back. The whole dance became a new thing as he held and led me, and I in turn felt and anticipated his every move.

As we danced, I realised, this is how God wants my relationship with Him to be. He is saying, 'Come closer, feel my every move, know the direction I am taking and move with me.'

A very dear friend, Lorrell, penned these words describing her relationship with her God:

Place your hand in mine my friend

Your thigh pressed close to me

And in the rhythm of our dance

Though the Storms Rage
Yet Will I Dance

I'll guide you to the end.[XI]

Another friend, Jacki wrote and recorded the song, *Beloved*. Part of that song says:

I delight in you my bride,

Your love for me, it makes me wild.

Come close and put your hand in mine,

Come dance for a while.

Look into my eyes and not at your feet,

Confusion will fade when you let me lead.[XII]

When Jesus was talking to His Father, just before he returned to Heaven, he prayed *'that all of them may be one, Father, just as you are in me and I am you. May they also be in us.'* John 17: 20, 21.

Revelation 19:7, 8 reads, '*Let us rejoice and be glad and give him glory! For the wedding of the Lamb has come, and his bride has made herself ready. Fine linen, bright and clean was given her to wear*'. (fine linen stands for the righteous acts of the saints) NIV

He is calling you and me, His bride, to come closer, to be one with Him. He is calling us to dance the bridal waltz with Him.

A Single White Daisy

I listened this morn to a song of love

Portrayed in "A Daisy a Day"

Of a love which reached beyond the grave,

The love of a man for his wife.

As he daily brought to her grave, his gift

Of a single white daisy for the rest of his life.

As I drove in my car to church this morn

I listened to the words of this song

And I thought of love and what it meant

Yesterday, today, and my whole life long.

I switched off the radio and tuned in to God.

As I dwelt on the gift of love,

The love between siblings, of kith and kin,

And God's love, gentle, as a dove.

There are so many different kinds of love,

Like the love between best friends,

Or the love for a special people group

Though the Storms Rage
Yet Will I Dance

Or for nations which reach the earth's ends.

And above and below and around and within

Each kind of love which is true

Is the everlasting, ever-reaching love of my God,

Portrayed in the vibrant rainbow's hue.

God's love is as immense as the universe

And as individual as His love for you.

It is seen in the stars and the sunset's glow

In a daisy's face, and the ocean, blue.

I listened this morning to a song of love

portrayed in 'a daisy a day'

And I drove to church and talked to my God

and thought of the love-bought choice.

Then stood in awe as a picture was shown

on the screen while we worshipped you

Of a single white daisy, my symbol of love and I

Knew, I had heard your voice."

Marion Kilchester

Chapter 8 ~ For Reflection

1. Can you recall a time when feeling totally alone and helpless, Jesus came to your aid?

2. God really loves you, as he does me, as indeed he loves everyone.

Write out John 3:16 putting your name into the verse:

'For God so loved me (your name) that he gave his one and only Son so that I (your name) shall not perish but have everlasting life'.

3. Do you remember a time when Jesus has reversed a bad time in your life? Maybe He has turned your mourning into dancing? Or maybe you are waiting for the change. If you are with someone you trust, then share how you feel and bring Jesus into your situation.

Each of us is Jesus' bride. He loves you so much, and has paid the supreme price for you.

Author's Notes

I have never written a book and I didn't want to revisit those difficult times in my life. For the first year after hearing God telling me to write, I wrote nothing. Then one day, I was asked by a pastor, "Marion, does 'dancing in the rain' mean anything to you?" I answered her question, and that night began to write.

As I wrote, I needed to revisit those extremely painful chapters in my life which up until then, I had safely filed away in the recesses of my memory, labelled 'Do Not Open'. I needed to face my fears, my grief, indeed every painful memory and write about it. In the writing, I knew that while I recalled the pain, I needed also to remember how I danced through each of those seasons in my life. I made myself vulnerable so that you can find healing, but the strange and wonderful thing is that I also received healing.

This then is my gift to you in the prayer that you too can learn to dance through the storms which life deals you. It is my prayer that you will come into a place of peace and a quiet resolution to live life well despite all.

Acknowledgements

I would like to thank Jo Wanmer for your encouragement to begin writing this book and for your continuing support, proofreading and for your endorsement. Thank you also for introducing me to Omega Writers

Thank you to Omega Writers for your friendship, knowledge and encouragement.

Thank you to Eileen Van Heerden for your patience, your listening ear and for typing up the first draft of my book.

Thank you to Natisha Ford for all the time you spent with me teaching me to use the computer and for doing things on the laptop which I couldn't. I could not have done this without you.

A big thank you to my editor, Nola Passmore for your invaluable advice and encouragement.

Thank you, Tim (my son), for doing my book cover.

Rick Aitchison, thank you for designing my webpage and getting it up and running for setting up my new laptop when my old one died, and for your extraordinary patience in teaching me how to master this new technology

Big thank you to Jo Wanmer, Louise Wakefield, Lorrell Preston and Sue Uhlmann for reading my book and giving me endorsements.

Many thanks to my family, and to my wonderful friends; Mary-Lou Worthington, Margaret Whittle and Jenny Tompkins for your input, support and encouragement.

About the author

I hope you enjoyed this book,
and that it has given you hope.

If you would like to contact me, order books, music or CD, you can follow my blogs or contact me at
www.leavesofhope.com.au

~ Marion ~

Marion Kilchester was born in Hurstville, Sydney. She grew up on a small farm near Tamworth, New South Wales. Marion became a piano teacher, examiner and a class-room music teacher. She has composed and published two books of music (arrangements/originals) which are listed in the Australian Guild of Music-Light Classical Recital Syllabus. She also recorded a CD of these pieces. She also completed a Diploma of Counseling and Group Work.

Marion currently resides in Queensland where she still teaches piano, at her home. She is Mum to three wonderful sons and Grandma to six beautiful grandchildren.

Testimonials

Writing with openness and honesty, Marion guides the reader into an illuminating life journey through tragedy, discovery and hope. In the darkness, the light is gently burning as a beacon, showing the way to the next open door.

*****Lorrell Preston*****

Diploma in Counselling at Christian Heritage College and spiritual director and affiliate member of the Quiet Garden Movement

Lorrell's home and garden provide space for quiet days and personal reflection for individuals and groups. She has enjoyed Marion's friendship for over twenty years.

It is always a delight to read someone's story. We get to know them closely as we travel the road through their account of a lifetime of joys and struggles. This is especially true when that time spent reading, encourages us to turn life's difficulties into strengths.

To read *Though the Storms Rage* is to be taken on a journey of the ups and downs of Marion's life. It is really an exploration detailing a discovery of dependance on God, the power of authentic friendships and the robustness these can bring to our lives. Reading of the ways God used His Holy Spirit to encourage, direct and guide Marion continually through the years is to reignite in our own lives the passion to constantly be in a place where we hear from God and obey.

When a person can look back and see that life's struggles can grow us stronger rather than bring defeat and take the time to share that with us, that story is worth reading. Refusing the temptation to have her future denied, Marion pursued her life in a determined, resolute way. This in turn should inspire and motivate us that we can, with help from God, bring not only ourselves but our families through to victory.

Sue Uhlmann

Associate Pastor, Destiny Church Caboolture

Bethel Sozo Australia Regional Facilitator

Whether we choose it or not, life brings storms. How we handle these storms is our decision. And our choices determine our future.

'Though the Storms Rage' is about dancing through those storms of life – whether it be a victory dance or a sideways two-step used to stay on our feet. Marion has weathered more storms than many of us – but she still dances, literally. Her decision to take up ballroom dancing in her sixties is a testament to her ongoing enjoyment of life.

I love Marion's stories and there are lots of them. This book is a gentle guided tour through her life. The stories are humble; the reactions real and honest. Storms batter and often bruise her. But she hangs on and we find her feet dancing again. This is real life.

It reminds me of her garden, 'The Garden of Hope', as she explains in the book. Marion's house stands tall on an acre of land. Every corner has been crafted and decorated with love. Walking through the garden, one is constantly surprised by another hidden treasure, a spot to sit, brilliant flowers, all with a live soundtrack of singing birds. There is grass flowing towards the creek, vines tumbling and flowering, trees towering above and pot plants on patios.

Marion's garden reflects her book. One can walk through the easy flowing commentary, and suddenly be pulled up by a vine climbing in an unexpected direction. Or one is drawn to a standstill to consider the unexpected, to ponder her responses and reflect on our own life experiences and decisions. Then one's eye is attracted by a flash of colour, a bold decision, a step of faith. Or one stumbles across an overgrown patch. The book doesn't hide the ugly or the undone, but owns it and finds a way through. The author's whole life could have been lived as a victim, but she shows us the way to walk in victory.

Read the book slowly. Allow time to ponder. Let the simplicity and wonder wash over you and bring you hope. Let it inspire you to lift eyes of faith above your storm and dance anyway!

Jo Wanmer

Author, pastor, and a friend of Marion's.

Jo has prayed through some of life's storms with Marion and is always delighted to see her emerge dancing. Her published book, Though the Bud be Bruised, *has bought healing and comfort to many. Other books are in various stages of completion.*

With her husband Steve, they are associate pastors of Access Church, Burpengary. It is a small group of passionate people spreading the Father's love across the nations.

This book is about Marion's struggles and her journey of overcoming negative events in her life to positively impact the lives of the many who are blessed to be around her. Marion has dedicated a portion of her life to develop a motivational book that moves the heart. She relays in a calm and positive manner all the difficulties that she has experienced from birth up to later in her life. The tone of the book leads the reader further as we are taken through the emotional roller coaster of painful events that make up Marion's challenging life, including parental relationship difficulties, the loss of her daughter, the birth of her son, her house burning down, ectopic pregnancy and family disagreements among others. The book is written in such a manner that generates heartfelt connection with the author. Marion has eloquently expressed her thoughts, emotions and challenges in a descriptive, pleasant story that is VERY much worth a read. I highly recommend this book for anyone who has experienced any challenges in their lives.

I was very blessed to have been able to read this book during its infancy and have found the content move me to tears and create strong visual imagery of the described events. I thoroughly enjoyed reading this book and would have no hesitations presenting the book, *Though the Storms Rage Yet Will I Dance*, and invite Marion to speak to other people that have experienced similar situations within their lives.

Throughout Marion's life she has proven to be a person of high moral character, strong determination, desire to encourage and support those around her and has a strong will to live an exceptional life.

I first met Marion in the beginning of the year 2016. During this time, I have seen Marion experience some of the challenges that she discusses in the book. Marion is an incredible inspiration to others. Even though Marion experiences traumatic challenges at times, Marion continually remains in an uplifted and positive mood. She has momentously impacted the lives of others around her through her work and her positive manner. She is certainly an inspiration to others. Even though Marion experienced harsh criticism since childhood, she has never given up on the goals, consistently strives to attain the highest standard, which is evidenced by her ability as an exceptional mentor and teacher, music writer and composer. It appears that no challenge is great enough for Marion. When she overcomes or attains one challenge she will focus on another challenge or goal and work her way through that goal until it also has been achieved to a high standard. If you at any stage have the opportunity to see Marion in person, I have no doubt you can also identify Marion's exceptional personality characteristics, inner strength and dedicated Christian attitude.

When you read this book, it is highly likely that you may develop some of your own inner strength and gain an increase in positive outlook with your own life. Enjoy this wonderful read.

Louise Wakefield
Provisional Psychologist

Notes

[I] Compassionate Friends
National Helpline: 1300 064 068
Queensland: (07) 3254 2657
www.compassionatefriendsqld.org.au
Compassionate Friends offers support to parents, grandparents and siblings who are grieving the loss of their child, brother or sister. They have support groups in every state, including regional areas. Telephone support is also available. When you ring the national helpline, you will be answered by a person in your state.

[II] *Each for the Other*, John W. Peterson Music Company.
All rights reserved. Used with permission.

[III] *Gaining Through Losing*, Evelyn Christenson 1980.
www.evelynchristensonministries.org
All rights reserved. Used with permission.

[IV] *Unknown*

[V] *Amazing Grace* is a Christian hymn published in 1779. Lyrics written by John Newton; music is of African American origin.

[VI] Definition of Paradox – a composite of the definitions given by the Collins English Dictionary:
www.collinsdictionary.com/dictionary/english/paradox
and Dictionary.com: www.dictionary.com/browse/paradox

[VII] *The Two Wolves*, also known as *"Grandfather Tells"* or *"The Wolves Within"*
www.firstpeople.us/FP-Html-Legends/TwoWolves-Cherokee.html

[VIII] *One Day at a Time*, Buckhorn Music 1973. Marijohn Wilkin and Kris Kristofferson. Used with permission.

[IX] Mahatma Ghandi; youtu.be/aq2XqaPqQuE

[X] Definition of Resilience, Yasmin Mogahed
www.azquotes.com/quote/1183949

[XI] *Not One Blemish*, Lorrell Preston.
All rights reserved. Used with permission.

[XII] *Beloved*, Jackie Horn.
All rights reserved. Used with permission.

www.ingramcontent.com/pod-product-compliance
Lightning Source LLC
Chambersburg PA
CBHW030253010526
44107CB00053B/1689